7/79 15

9 West

THE YOUNGER BROTHERS

The Attack on Flannery's House

THE YOUNGER BROTHERS

THEIR LIFE AND CHARACTER

By A. C. APPLER

With a Foreword by BURTON RASCOE

New York, Frederick Fell, Inc., Publishers

Designed by SIDNEY SOLOMON

PUBLISHED SIMULTANEOUSLY IN CANADA
BY GEORGE J. MCLEOD, LTD., TORONTO

Contents

Foreword

By BURTON RASCOE

To some eager young American folklorist and literary historian of the future, seeking to lay the foundation of a reputation as a specialist with a fascinating and unusual thesis for a Master's degree, I recommend the study of Augustus C. Appler and Appler's connection with the James and Younger families of outlaw fame and the methods pursued by him in gathering the material for his classic of American "folk-say" biography and conjectural history, *The Younger Brothers.*

For, although there is undoubtedly much fiction related guilelessly and with the best intentions by Appler in his obvious intention to depict the Younger brothers in the best light possible and to present actual or fabricated circumstances believed by him to be true, in extenuation of their manifest crimes, here is an extraordinary historical picture of a period, in particular of a certain, definite locality at a critical time of social, political and economic re-adjustments in the tragic decade for the Border States people following the Civil War.

Appler's book, indeed, is much more than a source book about the Younger brothers, pilfered indiscriminately and without credit by fictioneers and popular historians for sixty years, written while the outlaws were still alive, and written, for the most part, while they were still at large and wanted for more crimes than they could possibly have committed. It is also an on-the-spot local history of phases of the American Civil War that have never gotten into the official or academic histories, for the simple reason that the nefarious and bloody conflicts between the Kansas and Missouri irregulars (the Jayhawkers or Red Legs) on the Union side, and the Missouri, Indian Nations and Arkansas irregulars (The Bushwhackers), ostensibly on the Confederate side, had no official status or regular organizations and therefore made no official reports to the separate governments they allegedly represented and kept no official records that might be preserved and studied by historians.

Such official records that we do have in the archives of the Federal government in Washington and of the governments of the states have, necessarily, to do only with official Union dealings with the guerrillas, or irregulars, of both sides. These records obviously are scanty, incomplete, and tell only of one side of relatively unimportant events.

The records of the exploits of the Jayhawkers and Bushwhackers were necessarily kept in the heads of the separate participants. They came to light only in reminiscent accounts, told by survivors around family hearthstones, ten or fifty years after the event, retained in the memories of others, and retold, often with addenda from other sources, and elaborated with individual and borrowed fabrications, from which it is extremely difficult, if not impossible, to winnow all the authentic grains of truth.

Thus it is impossible for me either to authenticate or to refute with documentary evidence the thrilling and amaz-

ingly circumstantial account of the battle which Appler
calls "The Battle of Lone Jack," which is much more detailed and much more credible, in the simple matter of
human conduct in hand-to-hand fighting, than are the official accounts of battles by even such a graphic writer as
General Ulysses S. Grant in his magnificent *Memoirs*. So,
also, Appler's account of the enlistment of Indian troops
from various tribes, including Plains Indians along with
members of the Five Civilized Tribes, under Stand Watie
(whom Appler refers to as "Standwatie"), the Chief of the
Southern Cherokees and ranking Indian officer of the Confederate forces, although obviously gained at second-hand
and by ear from various sources, bears a remarkable aspect
of authenticity when Appler's account is read alongside
such reliable historical accounts of the Cherokee civil war
within the Civil War, as gathered from available records as
Morris L. Wardell's *A Political History of the Cherokee
Nation* and Grant Foreman's *The Five Civilized Tribes* and
A History of Oklahoma.

There is a sort of homely Homeric quality to Appler's
vivid and picturesque accounts of these guerrilla forays,
skirmishes and pitched battles; and nothing has been written that I know of that gives the reader a more intimate
sense of the personal emotions, hatreds, revengeful feelings
and sheer lust for carnage and destruction, or of the awful,
senseless depredations wrought upon farms and villages,
indiscriminately, by looting armed bands unofficially af-
filiated with both sides, as does this unskilled, semi-literate,
unverified record of events, set down by Appler as he gathered the details, here and there, with a Boswellian kind of
fervor.

(5)

All that I have been able to learn about Appler is deduced from his self-disclosures in his remarkable book. It is clear that he became a resident of St. Clair County some time during the early part of the year 1870, and I assume that he was a young journeyman printer from one of the Border States east of the Mississippi; that he had been too young to take any part in the Civil War but that his kinsmen definitely were on the Confederate side, for his sympathies were strongly with the Confederate cause in everything he wrote, even after the cause was irretrievably lost; and that, having served his printer's apprenticeship in some shop in Kentucky or Tennessee, he went to work on the *Osceola Weekly Democrat*, of which he subsequently became publisher and editor, as borne out by his designation on the title page of the earliest known edition of *The Younger Brothers*.

I gather, also from the text, that Appler began his account of the Younger brothers some time in the late winter or early spring of 1873, very likely under a subsidy from members of the Younger clan, possibly from Cole, Jim and Bob themselves, either as a whitewash job to make it easier for them to seek and get amnesty for their participation in the Southern rebellion and immunity from crimes known, or alleged, to have been committed by them, simply as members of the James and other outlaw gangs, or else as an alibi and cover-up for still further bank, stage, and train robberies which they expected to carry out in their careers, already dedicated to lawlessness and crime.

Certainly Appler gathered all the information he could about the Youngers, much of it from the boys themselves and from their numerous kin and friends in St. Clair, Jackson, Clay, Cass and Jasper Counties, Missouri. And he put it all down, just as he got it, without any chronological, or any other order, indeed, often relating events backward, chronologically, or jumping about in time with such a confusing lack of a sense of continuity that he must be read, at times, with the utmost care, in order not to get a very confused notion of what he has to tell.

Appler also had a habit of narrating events as he got them from irresponsible hearsay just as though he had been an eye-witness and was telling exactly what happened, whereas what he relates was clearly not witnessed by anybody whatever and what happened was merely somebody's guess. For instance, the account of the roadside murder of Col. Henry W. Younger, father of the famous brood of outlaw sons, is plainly fictional speculation. No one saw the murder; no one could honestly say that it was committed by a band of Jayhawkers, or that it was committed by a lone outlaw, or anything else about it. Appler relates that the leader of the band "knew" that the elder Younger was carrying a large sum of money and tells us just what went on in the mind of the leader; and also how the band took one sum of money from the murdered man but overlooked a large sum of money hidden in a belt around his body—all things which neither Appler nor anybody else could know from the facts as given.

I found that the way to read Appler with the greatest enjoyment and the most profit in credible information is to watch for those parts of his narrative wherein he gives factual accounts of happenings to which there could have been no witnesses and discount them, or ignore them, as mere hearsay gossip based upon, possibly, a tiny shred of

truth. Thus, also, the contradictions in his story can readily
be ironed out if the verifiable fact is juxtaposed with the
palpably invented fact.

It is obvious from the Laird & Lee text of *The Younger
Brothers,* published in 1892, that the book was first completed in March or April, 1875. For, Appler, in mentioning
the killing of John Younger, says that it occurred "a little
over thirteen months ago." John Younger was shot to death
by W. J. Allen, a Pinkerton detective, whose real name
appears to have been Lull, in a gun battle between John
and James Younger, on one side, and Pinkerton detectives
Boyle (alias Wright), Lull (alias Allen), and Edward B.
Daniels, on the other, in which Daniels was also killed, on
the dirt highway between Roscoe and Chalk Level, near the
Snuffer place, a few miles south of Monegaw Springs, St.
Clair County, Missouri, at about 2:30 in the afternoon of
March 16, 1874.

Appler says in his *Introduction,* which may be presumed
to have been written after the body of the book had been
completed and was ready for the printer, that he had been
working on the book for eighteen months, which means he
must have begun research in August or September, 1873.
The date has significance because on May 21 of that year
the James-Younger gang of outlaws, on the proposal and
plan of Jesse James had held up the Sainte Genevieve, Missouri, Savings Association Bank and had escaped with
$4000, without injury to anyone, and had followed this
exploit by "inventing" armed train robbery, by stopping
and boarding the Chicago, Rock Island and Pacific express
train, near Adair, Iowa, taking $3000 from the safe in the
express car and several hundred dollars in cash and jewelry

(*8*)

from the passengers, whom they lined up outside the train. That was on July 31, 1873. Since Cole and Jim Younger and Jesse and Frank James (with three others) were widely reported (on what turned out to be quite reliable authority, Jesse himself) to have participated in both crimes, the Younger brothers in September 1873, were very definitely "hot," in both usages of that convenient modern slang term: they were "hot" in the gangster or underworld use of the term, meaning that they were being eagerly sought by the "law"—the police were hot on the trail; and they were also "hot" in the journalistic use of the term, meaning they were sensational ("hot") news, good circulation-makers for newspapers and magazines and good sales potentials as subjects of books written about them.

From this I deduce that, say some time in August or early September 1873, either some publisher of the twenty-five-cent paper-backed books about outlaws, crime, and sin, which were very popular reading then, as now, in casting about for some one to write a book about the Youngers who presumably knew, or could learn, something fairly reliable about them, was told about, or hit upon, Augustus C. Appler of the *Osceola Weekly Democrat*. Or else Appler was approached by some member, or members, of the Younger clan, offering a subsidy of the composition and printing costs if he would write and print, at his own plant, a book designed to counteract the evil reputation the Youngers were getting everywhere by the flood of stories in newspaper dailies, in weeklies, in magazines, and in book quickies, purporting to give true accounts of their exploits, often fictional and absurd to a fantastic degree, picturing them as everything from a romantic band of modern Robin

Hoods to monsters of murder and depravity, akin to the infamous and mostly legendary Murel, whose trail of horrors was celebrated in picturesque language and with astonishing credulity by Samuel L. Clemens ("Mark Twain") in the papers he was writing for an Eastern newspaper syndicate in 1874-1875 which were later collected under the title *Life on the Mississippi.*

I can't rule out the conjecture that Appler might have been commissioned by a St. Louis, Chicago, or Cincinnati publisher of paper-bound books, or by the editor of a newspaper syndicate in New York, a few of which did a flourishing business in those days, supplying both daily and weekly newspapers with "boiler-plate" news features, travel accounts, and fiction serials, at low cost. The stuff was set up in regular newspaper column width and length; and stereotype mats were made and shipped out by mail to newspapers which cast their own plates from the mats, or else the plates were made from the mats and shipped by express or freight.

It was customary for these Eastern editors and publishers, notably the James K. Fox Co., publishers of *The National Police Gazette,* to have correspondents, free-lance or accredited, on weekly newspapers all over the country, from whom they got reams of stuff weekly, used only a fraction of what they received, and paid for it by the word, or line, as it appeared in print. Thus S. W. Harman of the Fort Smith (Arkansas) *Elevator,* a weekly, published at the seat of the Federal District Court during the time it was presided over by Isaac C. ("Hanging Judge") Parker, was correspondent for *The National Police Gazette;* "Eye Witness," who wrote the classic source book *The Daltons,* was pretty certainly a reporter on a Coffeyville, Kansas, weekly; and the author of the spurious *Life of John Wesley Hardin, as Written by Himself*, was very likely a reporter on the staff of an Austin, Texas, newspaper and a correspondent for *The National Police Gazette.*

The title page of the earliest known edition of *The Younger Brothers*, of which William F. ("Bill") Kelleher, probably the foremost living authority on Western Americana, tells me only four copies are known to exist, bears the copyright line, "Copyright MDCCCLXXV by Augustus C. Appler," which is one of the three copyright lines on the title page of the Laird & Lee edition of 1892; but that earlier edition was bound with, and second in position to, a book called *Border Outlaws of the West* by J. Duell, which has no title page, no copyright line and was published (as it now seems to have been established) by an unidentified firm in St. Louis in 1892, and immediately withdrawn, presumably on a threat of a suit in libel by some member of the James or Younger families. The part of the book by Duell was mostly about Frank and Jesse James, whose kin had successfully intimidated publishers into withdrawing scheduled or proposed books about the outlaw members of the two families hitherto. (Mrs. Frank James caused the withdrawal of a book on Frank and Jesse James by Frank Triplet in 1882, after winning a suit in libel against Triplet and his publisher and getting a court order restraining them against further distribution of the book.)

Just what happened to Appler's manuscript of *The Younger Brothers* after he had finished it in April or May, 1875, it is interesting to speculate about. The untitled, undated *Border Outlaws of the West* of 1892, would indicate that Appler had entered one copy of the book (which was all that was required at that time) and had sent a dollar to the Registrar of Copyright in 1875 for that "Copyright MDCCCLXXV by Augustus C. Appler" says so. But copyright procedure was very loosely regarded in those days and possibly Appler thought—as a lot of misguided writers think nowadays—that all that is necessary to copyright a work is to put "Copyright by So-and-So" on the title sheet of the manuscript.

At any rate, catastrophe struck and felled the whole notion and tenor of Appler's *The Younger Brothers*, making him and the book pretty ridiculous. For on September 7, 1876, just two years after he had begun his book and less than six months after he had finished it, the Northfield fiasco occurred: Cole, Jim and Bob Younger, Jesse and Frank James, Clell Miller, Charley Pitts and Bill Chadwell attempted to rob the First National Bank and were foiled in the attempt. Miller and Chadwell were killed, the three Younger brothers were riddled with bullets, captured, and jailed on charges of murder and armed robbery, while the James brothers, like scared jack-rabbits high-tailed it at the first sign of armed opposition, abandoned their stricken comrades, and departed for parts unknown.

This was a blow to Appler, because it was his contention throughout the book that the Youngers were nice, pious boys, who had been driven into a life of crime by the persecutions heaped upon them and their families and kin after the close of the Civil War, because of their misfortune of having been on the losing side; that, after one or two excursions in armed robbery, they had repented of their sins,

(*12*)

had resolved to commit no more crimes, and were hiding out in hope that the amnesty granted good citizens who had mistakenly fought against the Union would be honored concerning them, and they could settle down to peaceful and respected lives as the honest farmers they were at heart. But, wrote Appler, they are being hounded and accused of numerous crimes they had had no part in and could have had no part in, because of the time and distances which not only separated the crimes but also separated the scenes of the crimes, as scores of honest witnesses in St. Clair, Jackson and Clay counties would swear to. And, moreover, said Appler (and here he made the confident statement and the prediction which were subsequently to make him appear very foolish) the police and reward-seekers were taking their own lives in their hands and courting death, because the Younger boys were infallible deadshots and would never be taken alive and could not be, because no one was brave enough or could shoot accurately enough to disarm them.

As a matter of fact, it has been definitely established that, although both Jesse and Frank James were fair shots, but not crack-shots by any means, none of the Younger boys was either fast or accurate with a revolver, and that Cole was such a bad shot that, in an open duel at ten paces with a man much older than himself, in a Louisiana parish near Shreveport, Cole was slow on the draw, got hit in the leg and after taking deliberate aim at the man's heart, managed only to pink his adversary in the right shoulder. Both the Younger and James boys, from all the evidence about them that is verifiable, were brave only when they had all the advantages of weapons and place; they preferred shotguns to revolvers because of their scatter power at short distances;

(*13*)

and, being trained in guerrilla warfare, they relished most to shoot from ambush, or when the victim was unarmed, or had his back turned.

It would seem from the text that, for a time, while the Youngers were awaiting trial at the State penitentiary at Stillwater, Minnesota, the Youngers were considered "hot" news by some publisher and that Appler hastily wrote, possibly on order, an account of the Northfield fiasco as an additional chapter to his book about the Youngers. But even so, it is apparent that he did not, or rather could not, write the last paragraph of this chapter until he had got word that a jury had found the boys guilty of the charges in the Grand Jury indictment and that Judge Samuel Lord had sentenced them to imprisonment for the remainder of their natural lives.

But, it would appear, something happened to "Gus" Appler's manuscript about the Younger brothers even after he had fixed it up with a new chapter and some "miscellaneous" additional material—which seems to have been copied out of various weekly newspaper accounts of the doings of various outlaws of the time. It is "Bill" Kelleher's conjecture that, so powerful and, in general, so well-heeled financially and politically were the Younger and James clans and their friends and sympathizers, that editors and publishers, for a period of about fifteen years, were scared off from publishing anything whatever about the Youngers or the Jameses which tended to do otherwise than whitewash them; that threats of libel suits were frequent and persuasive whenever a book was announced about either of the clans, and the threats were not exclusively from Mrs. Frank James, or her blood kin, but from persons connected with other families who had reason to believe their family names would crop up in the accounts.

At all events, it seems that Appler's books did finally see print, but briefly, and in an extremely limited number of copies, in 1882, as the second part of a two-part book called *Border Outlaws of the West*, whereupon it disappeared for ten years, when one G. E. Wilson, apparently a printer-publisher in Chicago at the time—although his name does not appear among the many printers, publishers, editors, butchers, merchants, railroad men, architects, bankers, writers, poets, restaurateurs and professors in Felix Mendelsohn's monumental *Chicago and Its Makers* (1929)—decided to get in on the bonanza in publishing anything that had to do with William F. Cody, better known as "Buffalo Bill," who was the rage at the time.

In this year, 1955, people who contemplate the phenomenon of the "Davy Crockett" craze, which has been zooming ever since Walt Disney's epical film about the famous frontiersman, pioneer and scout, with its song about Davy, hit the movie theater and TV screens practically simultaneously, may think the craze is an unique and unparalleled thing. Actually there have been other crazes which have hit the country with just as great an impact, if not greater, since they have affected not only the youngsters but members of all generations. There was the "Trilby" craze in the 1880's and then there was the "Buffalo Bill" craze in 1890 to 1894.

Now, in 1890, many of the public-spirited millionaires of Chicago grew very self-conscious about the fact that Chicago was too widely known for its butchers and its slaughter-houses, its smells of cattle and glue-works from the boiling of cattle-hooves and bones, and for its shanty-town lake-front and its slums. They wanted to make the world know that Chicago was culture-conscious, a patron city of the arts, sciences and learning. So they decided to "make culture hum," as one Chicagoan put it, by staging a world's fair to top all world's fairs. They raised the money by public subscriptions, to which they doubled the ante by chipping in an equal amount among themselves for every dollar contributed by the public. Then they scheduled their fair to open in 1892, as the World's Columbia Exposition, in commemoration of the discovery of America by Christoforo Columbo.

The great popular attraction of the fair, quite aside from its cultural and scientific exhibits, was what they designated as *The Midway*, a sort of glorified Coney Island, with all sorts of side-show concessions, including the hootchie-cootchie dancer, billed as "Little Egypt," which, incidentally became the biggest "draw" of the whole exposition and about the only thing that oldsters, who saw the Fair, can remember about it.

But long before "Little Egypt" was granted a concession on *The Midway*, promoters of the World's Columbian Exposition—including Cyrus McCormick, the reaper king; Potter Palmer, the hotel tycoon; Harlow N. Higinbotham, the great merchant; Gustavus F. Swift and Philip Danforth Armour, the world's greatest butchers; Robert R. ("Bob") Lincoln, the martyred president's son, president of the Pullman Company; and other big-shots of the day petitioned "Bill" Cody, then the nation's entertainment favorite with his touring "Buffalo Bill's Wild West Show," to lead the parade on the day of the inauguration of the fair and to take, free of charge, the principal concession on *The Midway*.

Cody accepted, the joyous news was advertised, and toy, gimmick and souvenir manufacturing firms went into double-shift and overtime duty turning out "Buffalo Bill" items, from fringed shirts to toy pistols. And the twenty-five-cent publishers began to ransack their safes for unused manuscripts that might be turned into "Buffalo Bill" books. G. E. Wilson, obviously, didn't have any manuscript or book rights to anything about "Buffalo Bill," but he did have, it seems, proof sheets, plates, page proofs or something called *The Younger Brothers*.

Now there is nothing in *The Younger Brothers* about "Buffalo Bill" or about hunting buffalo or fighting Indians; the Youngers were Bushwhackers ostensibly fighting on the Confederate side during the Civil War, whereas William F. Cody was a heroic and gallant, if eccentric, officer in the Federal Army both during and after the Civil War.

But this did not deter Wilson. He went about the preparation of a "Buffalo Bill" book that would really be about the Youngers and called *The Younger Brothers*. The cover would take care of that; the cover, then as now in the twenty-five-cent reprint field, had nothing whatever (or very little) to do with the text; it was something to catch the eye and stimulate curiosity to the point of purchase.

But, again, Appler's book met an unhappy abortive fate. For the contractors finally concluded that it would be impossible for them to finish their lagoon-digging and palace-building and have everything ready by Columbus Day 1892; that the opening would have to be postponed until 1893. "Buffalo Bill," then, had to be counted out as the one to lead the inaugural parade and draw the crowds on *The Midway;* for he had already contracted for his tri-

(*17*)

umphal European Tour, where he and his sharpshooters, cowboys, and Indians were to appear before all the crowned heads, and start a cowboy craze in France which has survived to this day in the "Apache" hoodlums of Paris and the "Apache" dance. He contracted to return in 1893.

So Appler's *The Younger Brothers* was again shelved for a year, until the return of "Buffalo Bill" as the World's Fair's chief attraction, outside of "Little Egypt." By that time the publishing firm of Laird & Lee had taken over Wilson's rights in the Appler book. Unless it was Wilson who had commissioned the cover before them, they commissioned an artist to make a cover in black and white closely approximating a famous Frederick Remington equestrian portrait of "Buffalo Bill," which was used as a poster advertising Cody's wild west show.

This was the cover of the Laird & Lee edition of Appler's *The Younger Brothers,* published in Chicago in 1892 and bearing on the title page, the three copyrights—by Appler in 1875, by Wilson in 1891, and by Laird & Lee in 1892. The cover is of slick paper, oyster gray in color. At the top *The Younger Brothers* is printed in light orange. In the foreground there is the familiar triumphant Cody, seated in a western saddle on a rearing show-horse and lifting his wide-brimmed white stetson high over his head in salute to the paying customers. To the left, in the background, there is a pen drawing of a tepee of the type conventional with the Sioux and Blackfeet Indians, and four more smaller tepees receding into the background. Following Cody at a distance, are pen sketches of what appear to be an Army scout, two Federal cavalrymen of the plains service outfits, an Indian wearing a war-bonnet and on horseback, and a lone buffalo.

The drawing is unsigned but in the style of Remington.

(In order to convey some of the original flavor of the book, there is reproduced, in pen-and-ink version, on the jacket of the present edition the illustration which appears on the Laird & Lee cover.)

So it would appear that Appler's book about the Youngers did finally see the light in 1892-93, seventeen years after he finished writing it, and as a book somewhat fraudulently appearing to be a book about "Buffalo Bill." With the "Buffalo Bill" craze as yet unabated in 1893, Cody, the pride of the World's Columbian Exposition and a national hero akin to Davy Crockett in our time, it is reasonable to suppose that Appler's literary industry was at length rewarded, not by cash, to be sure, but by the appreciation of a great number of readers, who had bought the book along with other World's Fair souvenirs, including a rubber doll representing "Little Egypt," which did a belly-dance, if you squeezed and unsqueezed it in the right place.

I have found the Appler book reliably informative about many otherwise obscure or confusing points in the history of the Jameses and the Youngers, reticent upon precisely the matters I would expect the James and Younger clans to be reticent, and therefore in itself very revealing and dramatically rich in its portraiture of the issues, and how they were met and argued, which cleaved families, made mortal enemies of close friends, caused senseless arson and property destruction as well as death and spread disablement and direst poverty throughout a hitherto richly fertile countryside for years after the war which had divided the country.

After several careful readings of this book and after

much checking and rechecking, I have become all the more firmly fixed in some earlier conclusions which I reached while I was writing *Belle Starr; The Bandit Queen.* Among those conclusions are: that (1) the Youngers and the Jameses were cousins but that the families were also interrelated by ties of marriage, and that their principal partners in their forays, such as the men known as Chadbourne and Miller, were close kinsmen also, either by blood or marriage; (2) that the Youngers and the Shirleys, from whom Belle Shirley Starr sprang, were neighbors and friends, though not related by blood, at some time before Belle Shirley's father opened his hotel in Carthage, to be exact, that when the Youngers lived on a farm a little to the southwest of Lee's Summit, Jackson County, Missouri, they were at least acquainted with the Shirleys who lived on a farm on the Independence-Carthage highway, which skirted both farms, not so many miles south of the Younger place that they might not have sold their produce at the same markets; (3) that when Cole, Jim and Bob Younger bought a place in Scyenne, Dallas County, Texas, in 1868, as he relates in a letter of Appler, it was on the advice of John Shirley, Belle's father, who had bought a piece of land in the same section in 1863 or 1864, and that while there, Belle, who was 20 in 1868 and Cole, who was 24, became lovers, the issue of which was Belle's illegitimate child, who she named Pearl Younger; that the legend about the marriage to Jim Reed on horseback by a preacher on horseback, when Belle was allegedly head of an outlaw gang and they were "on the scout," very likely masks an actual incident of a mock marriage, performed as a joke during or after some spree, with Belle and Cole as the principals; (4) that Cole's denial in

(*20*)

Stillwater prison that he had ever loved, visited, or courted
Belle but knew of her and her family, was an inveterate,
natural, and inevitable response of the Southern male,
outlaw or judge, convict or congressman concerning any
woman with whom he had had sexual relations, it being
an inviolable part of an unwritten code about which the
Southerner is usually strangely superstitious; (5) that, although Belle did apparently marry Jim Reed, subsequently
and, after his death, married Sam Starr under the Cherokee
tribal laws, by virtue of which she was automatically dealt
60 acres of the tribal lands adjoining Sam's, she remained
more or less in love with Cole to the day of her death,
sentimentally naming the bend of the South Canadian River
in the Cherokee Nation, within the loop of which she and
Sam had their log cabin, Younger's Bend, calling her first-
born, a girl, Pearl Younger, and making other manifesta-
tions of an attachment to the memory of Cole. I was once
attracted by the notion that Bob Younger was the father of
Pearl and that Bob was for a time Belle's lover, a reference
to which had prompted the story of Cole's duel with James
White, allegedly prompted by White's insulting references
to a "girl Bob was in love with"; but I ruled that notion
out, on figuring that Bob was younger than Belle, which
was enough in itself for me to scratch off the possibility that
she was in love with him. Cole's account of the reasons for
the gunplay with White is clearly fictitious, for, in the code,
it was Bob's duty to defend his sweetheart's honor, not
Cole's, even if Cole had to force him to do it; and that would
be precisely the sort of evasion to which Cole would resort
in order to keep Belle's name or the name of any other
woman out of the affair in talking about the duel; (6) I

cannot accept Carl W. Breihan's contention in his otherwise admirable and marvellously authenticated *The Complete and Authentic Life of Jesse James* (Frederick Fell, Inc., New York, 1953; $4.50) on two points, namely (1) that Cole never knew Belle Starr personally, a statement made by Breihan on the authority of an unnamed St. Louis police officer, who allegedly got the information from the lips of Cole himself, when he had taken Cole in and sobered him up after a drunken spree, or (2) that it was Frank James, not Jesse, who held the revolver at the temple of bank cashier Heywood's head and shot him dead during the robbery attempt at Northfield; for Breihan again gives as his authority the unnamed police officer who told Breihan he heard this from Cole's lips, whereas Breihan's own account of the Northfield disaster does not jibe with this, and, indeed, not only does not place Frank inside the bank at the time of the murder, but also says he was very drunk that afternoon—a circumstance alone that would have caused either Cole or Jesse to forbid Frank to enter the bank where alertness, perfect coordination, and coolness were of the essence in the robbery plan.

Because my own copy of the Laird & Lee edition of Appler's *The Younger Brothers* is fast crumbling to dust and pieces by the disintegration of the poor quality paper on which it was printed, and because I imagine all other copies of this rare edition of an undeniable classic of Americana to be in a like condition, I congratulate Frederick Fell, Inc. upon its enterprise in giving this classic a handsome new life, well-printed on durable paper, but preserving the original text exact, including misspellings, typographical errors and errors of grammar and syntax.

(Even the original pen-and-ink illustrations are here reproduced exactly as they appear in the original.)

Appler's invaluable jottings-down of original historical research, his patient questionings of people who knew the Youngers, and his industry in writing to preachers and prominent citizens in remote parishes of Louisiana and remote towns in Missouri and Arkansas for verification of Cole Younger's naming them for his alibis—all this, plus his individual contribution to the local history of the Jayhawker-Bushwhacker internecine warfare of irregulars, deserves its chance with posterity, particularly since it had the darndest time ever getting printed at all.

New York City
August 16, 1955

Introduction

In presenting the public with a work of this character the author deems it unnecessary to offer an apology for its appearance. The names of the principal characters herein mentioned, the Younger Brothers, are familiar to every reader of newspapers throughout the country. This volume is not a romance, drawn from imagination, but a plain, unvarnished history of facts and incidents that have actually occurred, the names herein given being real, not fictitious, and nearly all of whom are living at this time.

The author of this book has been a resident of St. Clair county, Missouri, the past four years. This county is, or at least has been partially the home of the Younger Brothers, ever since the late war, and at the present time they have many relatives and intimate friends residing here, with most of whom I am personally acquainted, and from whom I have obtained much of the subject matter in this book. I have also had several interviews with the Younger Brothers, in regard to the various charges against them. I have devoted much time during the past eighteen months in getting up this history, ever keeping in view truth and impartiality. But few persons know the whereabouts of the Younger Brothers at any time, where they go or when they will return. And those who have their confidence seldom allow themselves to be drawn into conversation about them. Thus it will be seen that it is no easy matter to obtain reliable information in regard to them.

It is not my desire or wish to shield these men from any depredations they may have committed, or to in the least influence public opinion in their favor, but simply to give facts and incidents in connection with their lives, leavng the public to judge for themselves of the manner of men they are, and of their guilt or innocence of the many crimes charged against them.

As the reader is aware, almost the entire newspaper press of the country has, from time to time, during the past few years, devoted much time and space to these notable characters, while many of the articles which have found their way into the columns of leading journals throughout the country, North, South, East and West, were the grossest misrepresentations. Every species of rascality and deviltry committed in Missouri and adjoining States, has either been charged upon them directly, or they were accused of belonging to the band of outlaws who perpetrated the crimes, and shared in the spoils, while it was known to many persons in Missouri and elsewhere, that the Younger Brothers were hundreds of miles away from the scenes of lawlessness at the time, and were innocent of any complicity in the crime. That these men are brave and daring fellows, no one acquainted with them will deny. It cannot be said that they court danger, but never avoid it when fairly met. Their lives, from early boyhood, have been one continued series of hairbreadth and miraculous escapes, many times receiving serious and dangerous wounds, barely escaping with their lives.

A little over twelve months ago one of these boys, John
Younger, was killed in an encounter with two of Pinkerton's Chicago Detectives, near Monegaw Springs, St. Clair
county, Missouri. From that time until the present, at
least so far as the public have had any knowledge of them,
the Younger Brothers have not been in any difficulty, and
but little has been said about them, save that they were
seen in different parts of the country, yet when the reader
comes to peruse this work he will find that for several
months thereafter the remaining three brothers were engaged in almost every-day fighting, having been pursued
and hunted down like wild beasts. These facts we gathered
from one of their most intimate friends, to whom the
boys related their trials and difficulties.

In the preparation of this work, at times, we have
endeavored to give, as near as possible, the exact language
of the boys in relating incidents in their lives, making it
just what it is intended to be, a plain, unvarnished history
of things that occurred during and since the war. The
intimate friends of these boys have always claimed that
they did nothing more than what was either forced upon
them by personal enemies, or resulted from bad feeling
growing out of the late war—the murdering of their
father in cold blood, by a band of Jayhawkers, and then
robbing him of a considerable amount of money; the
brutal and inhuman treatment received by their widowed
mother, &c.

Three of these boys are still living, namely, Thomas
Coleman, James Henry and Robert Ewing Younger.

In conclusion, believing that the public mind was ripe
for a reliable work of this kind, this volume is presented.

The leading characters are the Younger Brothers, yet the reader will find that other noted persons are referred to, such as Quantrell, a famous bushwhacker during the war, the James Boys, Arthur McCoy, &c., and, taken together, will go to make up much of the unwritten history of the late war, both in Missouri and Kansas, as also the leading incidents of outlawry the past six years in the West.

The author of this work possesses facilities for obtaining reliable information in regard to the Younger Brothers, enjoyed by but few, and much of the matter herein contained was sketched by Cole Younger himself, and merely written out more in detail. This is the only work giving the lives of these men ever published.

THE AUTHOR.

Osceola, St. Claire County, Mo.

Henry W. Younger.

Col. Henry Washington Younger, father of the Younger Brothers, was born in Crab Orchard, Kentucky. He moved to Missouri with his father when quite a young man, settling in Jackson county. About the year 1830 he married Miss Busheba Fristo. The union thus formed proved a happy and contented one, both parties being greatly attached to each other, and they raised a very large family of children, fourteen in number, eight girls and six boys. All, saved three, lived until they grew to womanhood and manhood.

Col. Younger figured conspicuously in politics, and was for a number of years Judge of the County Court of Jackson Co., and at one time a member of the Missouri Legislature.

The names of the boys who lived to the age of majority were Richard, Thomas Coleman, James Henry, John and Robert E. Younger. All but two of the girls reached womanhood and nearly all married men of standing and wealth, four of whom are now living in different parts of the country.

Col. Henry W. Younger continued to reside in Jackson county, Missouri, until 1858, when he moved near Harrisonville, in Cass county, Missouri. He was a very active business man. He dealt largely in stock, was quite an extensive farmer, and largely engaged in merchandising. In 1861 he had a large livery stable in Harrisonville, and owned some of the best blooded stock in the west. He was very successful in business, and at the time of his death was thought to be worth over $100,000, which, at that time was considered, in that section of country, a very wealthy man. He owned two large and highly improved farms, one of about 600 acres in Jackson county, ten miles south of Independence, Missouri, and one adjoining the town of Harrisonville, in Cass county, Missouri. He also carried on merchandising in Harrisonville.

When the war broke out Col. Younger was a staunch Union man. The Kansas troubles, a few years previous to the late "unpleasantness" between the Northern and Southern States, created considerable ill-feeling between the citizens on the borders of Kansas and Missouri, growing out of the attempt, on the part of Missourians, to make Kansas a slave State. This sectional feeling continued to ripen and increase, from year to year, and the breaking out of the war caused an open rupture all along the line between those States. The Missourians who took part in this matter were termed Guerrillas, while those of Kansas were designated Jayhawkers. The Jayhawkers, as is well known, were headed by Jim Lane, Jennison, Montgomery, Anthony, etc., whose names, years ago, before the late war, were familiar to the country. To the Guerrillas, anything across the Kansas border was lawful prey, while the Jayhawkers of Kansas knew no distinction among the people of Missouri. With the echo of the first gun fired on Fort

Sumpter, the dogs of war were let loose all along the Missouri and Kansas border. Jennison and his band of Jayhawkers went through Jackson and other border counties of Missouri, sacking and burning, while the Missourians, under the lead of Quantrell, finally sacked and burned the town of Lawrence, Kansas.

Jennison, in one of his raids into Missouri, passed through Jasper, Jackson and Cass counties, going as far as the town of Harrisonville, at which time he sacked and burned most of the town, then the home of Col. Henry W. Younger, who, although a firm Union man, was one of Jennison's special victims. Several thousand dollars worth of vehicles from his extensive livery stable were carried off, and forty head of blooded horses were confiscated, making his loss on this single occasion about $20,000. Col. Harry Younger, however, managed to escape the clutches of the Jayhawkers.

From that time on, Col. Younger was shadowed from place to place, and being a very wealthy man, who usually carried with him large amounts of money, the Jayhawkers intended, the first opportunity, to murder and rob him. About the first of September, 1862, it became known that he would come into possession of a considerable amount of money, and that he was to go to Independence on a certain day to get it and bring it to Harrisonville. He went, in his buggy, at the appointed time, and parties laid in wait for him to return. Accordingly, when near Harrisonville, he was halted by about ten men, shot dead in his buggy, then robbed and left lying in the road. Previous to starting, Col. Younger had taken the precaution to place in his belt, which he carried buckled around his body underneath his clothing, all of his money except four hundred dollars, which he placed in his pocketbook. This the Jayhawkers got, not supposing he had any more with him. When his murder became known, the body was given in charge of his wife, and on preparing it for decent burial, the remainder of his money was found in the belt where he had placed it, which was taken charge of by his wife.

At another time the widow, and mother of a large family of children, was forced to fire her own house with her own hands at midnight, the flames arising from which lit up the road as the Jayhawkers rode off. From that time on, the Youngers were considered outlawed; one of the boys, Thomas Coleman Younger, shortly after joining the forces of Quantrell, and making it lively for Jayhawkers wherever he came across them.

After the burning of the house in Cass county, the mother gathered together her small children in a mere shanty in Lafayette county, Missouri, where she passed the winter. The Jayhawkers followed her trail as hunters would that of a she wolf and her cubs. One night they surrounded the shanty, with the hope of finding the older boy, Thomas Coleman, at home, and failing in that, they chased into the brush the next oldest, James Henry, then only fourteen years of age.

From Lafayette county the remaining helpless members of the family were driven into Clay county. Finally, shortly after the close of the war, the mother sickened and died, the result of the troubles and trials she had undergone.

Richard Younger.

Richard Younger was the oldest son of Henry W. Younger. He died in Jackson county, Missouri, in 1860, and was buried with Masonic honors, being a worthy member of the brotherhood, aged about 23 years. He died shortly after graduating, and those who knew him, regarded him as a very promising young man, and one who possessed considerable ability for his age. Had he lived, he, doubtless, would have endured many of the trials and hardships which fell to the lot of his younger brothers. For resentment is characteristic of human nature, and it is not reasonable to suppose that, had he lived, he would have sat quietly by and seen or known of his father being ruthlessly murdered and robbed, by a band of Jayhawkers; his mother insulted, abused, and compelled to fire her own house, driven from place to place, and at length filling an untimely grave, without resenting some of the wrongs that were committed upon his parents. Such would be human nature.

Thomas Coleman Younger.

Much has been said and written about the person whose name heads this chapter. The newspapers of the country have contained column after column, the productions of correspondents and editors, who gave what was claimed to be the whole unvarnished truth, while the reading public eagerly grasped after everything written and published about him. Thousands, it is to be presumed, imagined in their own minds what sort of a creature he must needs be. Indeed, we have seen men who, we thought, had more and better sense, assert that they would as soon meet a grizzly bear as Cole Younger; and men have actually avoided passing through St. Clair county, Missouri, for fear they would meet some of the Youngers. These things very much remind one of the imaginations of persons living East, some twenty-five or thirty years ago, who never were West, who could not believe that in the great West there were any real comforts and enjoyments; who imagined that there was an Indian lurking behind every tree or rock, with rifle or bow and arrow in hand, ready to shoot down every white man that dared to venture across the Mississippi river, West; who could not believe but what the white people who were then living West, were more like wild beasts than human beings, roaming over the wild prairies in search of the buffalo and deer, clothed only in the skins of wild animals, and who could relish raw meat as well as civilized and intelligent people meat that was properly cooked and prepared. Thousands there are at the present day, who can well remember these things, and we have no doubt there are thousands still living, who have never been West, who have very erroneous ideas of Western life and Western people; who cannot properly realize the fact that in the great West we have large and handsome cities, possessing every advantage and every facility for enjoyment and pleasure, and in which are stores that would be a credit and ornament to any Eastern city, filled with the most costly articles of merchandise. In fact the West is the place to find every convenience and luxury the world affords. Those who doubt the truth of this, we advise to come West and see for themselves.

A few months since a Chicago paper contained quite a lengthy account of the cruel manner in which Cole Younger was treated by the Jayhawkers at Harrisonville, Cass county, Missouri, in 1861. The whole story was one of wild imagination, without the least semblance of truth in it. Cole Younger never was captured during the war, neither was he ever hung up, whipped, or harmed in any way, although he would, undoubtedly, have been killed, had he not left home the very day he did.

Cole Younger remained at home until the fall or winter of 1861, when Neugent's men were stationed at Harrisonville, in Cass county, Missouri, having up to this time taken no part or lot in the war that was then going on. He frequently visited parties where the Missouri State

Militia were, and all went pleasantly and smoothly along. At one of these parties, however, which was held at the house of Col. McKee, a little jealousy seemed to spring up between Cole Younger and a militia Captain named Irvin Walley. A sister of Cole Younger, who was present at the party, refused to dance with Walley, which nettled him very much. Cole Younger, on this occasion, seemed to enjoy himself very much, more than usual, and monopolized the time and attention of the belle of the evening, much to the chagrin and mortification of Walley, who conceived the idea that because he ranked as a militia Captain he was superior to any citizen or common soldier. Walley seemed uneasy the whole evening, and showed signs of a determination to create a difficulty with Cole Younger. Finally, Walley was heard to make the remark that "Soldiers would stand no chance until they took that d——n Younger boy out." This information being told to Younger, he became satisfied that his presence was creating bad feeling, and that he was not wanted there, and he finally withdrew and went home, hoping thereby to avoid a difficulty, and thus be enabled to remain at home, assist his father in business and keep clear of the war. Even after he left the house Walley seemed not to be satisfied, but threatened death to Cole Younger.

When Cole Younger reached home he told his father what had happened, and said he feared the end was not yet, as Walley seemed determined to have a difficulty. His father then advised him to go down on the farm in Jackson county and raise a crop, thinking that when there he would be secure from the enmity of Walley, and be able to live in peace.

The following night Walley and a party of his men went to the house of Col. Henry Younger and made some violent demonstrations, threatening to "Show Cole Younger how the dancing went," but Cole had left that day, and thus in all probability, avoided being killed, or killing some one.

Capt. Walley soon learned that Cole Younger had gone to Jackson county, and at once determined to report him as having joined Quantrell, thus hoping to get up an excuse to perpetrate some deviltry and accomplish what he desired. As the sequel afterwards proved, the object of Walley was to stir up strife and give him an excuse for robbing Col. Harry Younger, father of Cole. All this time Cole Younger was busily engaged on the farm in Jackson county, not suspecting trouble or danger. But he was not long to remain in peace and quietude, and at length learned that he was being hunted down by Capt. Walley, who had reported him as being with Quantrell. He felt satisfied that Walley would endeavor to come upon him sometime when he was not suspecting danger, and probably murder him in cold blood. Finally, one day he learned that Walley, with his company of Missouri State Militia, was then on the way from Harrisonville to Jackson county, intending, as it had been given out, to capture Cole Younger, a noted bushwhacker. Younger, at this time, was inexperienced in war, and could devise no better means of escaping the clutches of Capt. Walley than to take to the brush, well knowing that he could keep out of his way, if nothing else. He also hoped that Neugent's men would be removed in a short time, and that then his troubles would end. He was without arms, and of course was unable to do harm. In this condition, young, inexperienced, and having

(*38*)

no ill-will towards any one, he managed to secrete himself among his relatives for some two or three weeks. During this time Colonel Younger, his father, was endeavoring to settle the pretended difficulty, (on the part of Walley,) between him and Cole, so that Cole could come home and remain in peace and quiet. But Neugent and Walley were both intent on plunder, and well knowing they could make no reasonable excuse for robbing Col. Harry Younger, who was a staunch Union man, they resolved to make a scape-goat of Cole and drive him to desperation, thereby finding a poor apology of an excuse for robbing the old gentleman, who was thought to be the wealthiest man in that section of the State, and at all times having considerable money on his person and about his house.

One day Capt. Walley went to the livery stable of Col. Harry Younger and hired a buggy and pair of fine match horses, promising to return them in a day or two. After gaining possession of them he refused to give them up, and appropriated the whole outfit to his own use. Almost simultaneous with this movement, a raid was made on Younger's Jackson county farm, for the purpose, as it was given out, of capturing Cole Younger, but really with the view of plunder. Cole was not there, at least they did not find him, but they did not hesitate to drive off all the stock and set fire to the grain bins. Col. Harry Younger made but little complaint after the loss and destruction of his property, but continued to manifest a great desire to make some disposition of Cole that would save trouble, as he well knew that if the boy once became thoroughly aroused, already observing that the "tiger" was being developed in him, that serious consequences would follow. His father

(*39*)

advised him to remain quiet and he would yet make some disposition of him to keep him out of trouble. He told his father that he "was tired of running like a wild beast, and would not do it much longer without hurting some one." The old gentleman then suggested that he had better go to school. To this Cole assented.

At once arrangements were made with that object in view, and clothing and the usual outfit prepared for him. Col. Younger named his plan of keeping Cole out of trouble to a friend in Kansas City, and was surprised to learn that his intentions had been anticipated and were known. His friend informed him that he was closely watched, and advised him not to attempt it, as it might result fatally to himself. On his return home Col. Younger informed Cole of these facts, and then, for the first time, he seemed fully aroused, saying, "It's all right, I will fight them awhile, then!"

He Joins Quantrell.

Cole Younger had frequently heard of Quantrell, and at once determined to risk his chances with him, and immediately started in search of his camp, finding him on the Little Blue, in Jackson county, Missouri. He went without arms, but remained only a short time before a fight occurred, at which time he succeeded in getting arms from a dead Federal. Thus, on the 20th of April, 1862, Coleman Younger was, for the first time, an armed soldier.

Joins the Confederate Army.

Early in the fall of 1864, during the last raid of Gen. Price into Missouri, Cole Younger joined the Confederate Army and went South with Price on his return. He was afterwards elected Captain of a company, and the following winter took his men and went into Louisiana, where he remained until the close of the war, which was in the spring of 1865.

Goes to Mexico.

After the close of the war Cole Younger and fifteen of the men belonging to his company went to Mexico. After remaining in Mexico about two months, he and several of the men sailed for California, the others taking the overland route for the same point. Cole remained in California until the fall of 1866, when he returned to the States, stopping in Jackson county, Missouri, near Blue Mills, on the farm of his mother, and went to work making rails, the greater portion of the fencing having been destroyed during the war. John and Robert were at home when he arrived, but James had not yet returned, having been captured in Kentucky with Quantrell, at the time Quantrell was mortally wounded and captured. James returned shortly afterwards, however, and all the boys went to work to fix up the farm.

At Home.

As previously mentioned, Cole Younger returned home from California in the fall of 1866, as did also James. They had not been home long until the Missouri Militia, together with the Kansas Jayhawkers, who then held all the offices in the border counties, began to organize into bands or Vigilant Committees, as some termed them, for the purpose of intimidating those of the opposition, and

(41)

eventually driving them from their homes. Their ears were continually assailed with threats of murder and mob violence. By the following spring it become absolutely dangerous, for Cole Younger especially, to stay at home, and he then left and went to Lee's Summit, in order to be out of the way and avoid assassination. Becoming tired of loitering around town idle, shortly afterwards he went to Louisiana, where he remained during the summer of 1867. In the meantime, James, John and Robert remained at home and cultivated their mother's farm.

In the fall Cole, thinking that probably the bitter feeling against him had subsided, returned home and went to work on the farm. He built his mother a house, fixed the place up as best he could, and prepared to live with her the remnant of her days. Cole bore no ill-will toward any one, and was willing to "bury the hatchet" and forget the past. But not so with his enemies. There was but a short respite. The old and bitter feeling against Quantrell's men, the "bushwackers," as they were commonly called, began to manifest itself in acts of violence. As heretofore mentioned, all the offices of honor, profit or trust, under the then semi-civil, semi-military rule in the border counties, were held by Kansas Jayhawkers and the old Missouri State Militia, of Neugent's regiment. These men nursed a deadly hatred against every one of Quantrell's men, especially against those who were most prominent and officers, such as Cole Younger had been. The Jayhawkers, under the shadow of official authority, committed murder with impunity. This gave them a fine opportunity to take revenge upon their personal enemies, and they improved the opportunity. They murdered William, commonly called

"Bill" Reynolds, Al. Shepherd, and others of Quantrell's men. They arrested George Maddox and Paine Jones, sent them to Lawrence, Kansas, and incarcerated them in a filthy jail for many months, without a shadow of a charge against them, except that they had served under Quantrell and followed his fortunes through the war. Dick Burns was murdered, and Bill Hulse was shot down while at work in a harvest field, and left for dead. Thus, one by one, Quantrell's men were disposed of, until it was apparent that there would be none left to tell the tale. At length there was organized at Pleasant Hill, in Cass county, a company of those Jayhawkers, under the command of one Timberlick, a Kansas red-leg, and who was at the time acting as Deputy Sheriff, under one R. S. Judy, one of Neugent's militia, and who had an implacable hatred against Cole Younger. The company was made up of the very worst men in that vicinity; men who were ever ready to perpetrate almost any crime, murder not excepted. They designed to capture, and doubtless murder, Cole Younger. They passed through Lee's Summit one day, creating a reign of terror in that little town, and went to the widow Wiginton's and took her son George, another of Quantrell's men, abused him shamefully, and then took him along with them as a guide and decoy, through whom they hoped to capture Cole Younger. Fortunately for him, and perhaps for some of them, Cole was not at home at the time, but three miles away, at the house of his brother-in-law. They then abused the family and compelled them to get supper for them, after which they left, taking with them John Younger, then a mere boy, whom they thought they could force to tell the whereabouts of Cole Younger. They threw

(*43*)

a rope around his neck, beat him with their pistols, and otherwise maltreated him, yet they failed to force him to give them any information. Such treatment as this is what forced James and John to leave home.

Another similar attempt to capture and murder Cole Younger was made by a party hailing from Independence, with a like result. Cole saw that it was impossible for him to live at home in peace. And the other boys had been so ill treated that they, too, were afraid to stay at home, and finally Cole took the other two boys, James and John, and started for Texas, where he prepared a home for his mother and sister, to which he intended to remove them, together with a black woman, Sue, who had remained faithful and true to them through all their trials and troubles, and is, to this day. In the meantime their mother, who was not able to go to Texas with them, and who never did recover from her illness, consumption, had to break up housekeeping, and, with her little girl and negro woman, went to live with her son-in-law, where she finally wasted away, and died at the residence of Lycurgus Jones, in June, 1870, while her sons were far away preparing a home for her in her old age.

Coleman and James returned during the summer and took their sister and the negro woman to Texas, where we shall leave them for the present.

In February, 1875, Thomas Coleman Younger was 32 years of age.

Fight at a Horse Race in Louisiana.

In 1869 Cole Younger, in the course of one of his roving freaks, found himself in one of the interior parishes of Louisiana, and attended a horse race. The great, gaunt, awkward Missourian had money with him, the result of a successful cattle speculation. The crowd intuitively recognized the presence of the money, and fixed upon Cole Younger for their prey. They badgered him, pressed around him with sharp words, and finally forced the borderer into the horse race. Younger had one of the famous long limbed, blue grass breed of racers, an animal not fair to look upon, but of great speed and bottom. He put every dollar he had upon his horse—$700. The money was placed in the hands of a storekeeper close by the track. All the time that Younger was preparing for the race, the crowd pressed around, flinging insulting epithets and abusive suggestions at their victim. The Missourian muttered a request that they should wait until after the race for the shooting to begin, but the crowd paid no attention. Finally Cole Younger announced his readiness, and at the word the horses were off. As they came in on the last quarter, Younger's horse was four lengths ahead, when out from the crowd sprang one of the bullies with a wild yell and flaunted in the face of the winning steed a cloth. The horse swerved, lost his stride, and came in second. Younger's light blue eyes glistened a little, but he said not a word. He dismounted, groomed his horse, and then, remounting, rode to the stakeholder and said: "You saw what happened, and don't mean to give that fellow my money." With an imprecation, the man in league with the crowd replied that he did. "Then," said Cole Younger, "the shooting has commenced." The crowd had gathered about him, laughing at his defeat, and hooting in derision. Out from their holsters came two dragoon revolvers, and with one in each hand Cole Younger emptied them with inconceivable rapidity into the mob and then, without waiting to see the effects, dashed away. Three of the crowd were killed outright, two died of their wounds, and five carry to this day, if they are all living, the scars of that terrible revenge.

Writes a Letter Vindicating Himself.

The Pleasant Hill, Missouri Review, of the 26th of November, 1874, contained the following letter from Thomas Coleman Younger, in which he endeavors to vindicate himself from the charges made against him, as follows:

HIS LETTER.

"DEAR CURG:—You may use this letter in your own way. I will give you this outline and sketch of my whereabouts and actions at the time of certain robberies with which I am charged. At the time of certain bank robberies, I was gathering cattle in Ellis county, Texas, cattle that I bought from Pleas Taylor and Rector. This can be proven by both of them; also by Sheriff Barkley and fifty other respectable men of that county. I brought the cattle to Kansas that fall and remained in St. Clair county until February. I then went to Arkansas and returned to St. Clair county about the first of May. I went to Kansas where our cattle were, in Woodson county, at Col. Ridge's. During the summer I was either in St. Clair, Jackson or Kansas, but as there was no robbery committed that summer, it makes no difference where I was.

The gate at the fair grounds in Kansas City was robbed that fall. I was in Jackson county at the time. I left R. P. Rose's that morning, went down Independence road, stopped at Dr. Nolan's and got some pills. Brother John was with me. I went through Independence, from there to Ace Webb's. There I took dinner and then went to Dr. L. W. Twiman's. Staid there until after supper, then

(*46*)

went to Silas Hudspeth's and staid all night. This was the day the gate was robbed at Kansas City. Next day John and I went to Kansas City. We crossed the river at Blue Mills, and went upon the other side. Our business there was to see E. P. West. He was not at home, but the family will remember that we were there. We crossed on the bridge, stayed in the city all night, and the next morning we rode up through the city. I met several of my friends; among them was Bob Hudspeth. We then returned to the Six-mile country by the way of Independence. At Big Blue we met James Chiles and had a long talk with him. I saw several friends that were standing at or near the gate, and they all said they didn't know any of the party that did the robbing. Neither John nor I were accused of the crime for several days after. My name would never have been used in connection with this affair, had not Jesse W. James, for some cause, best known to himself, published in the Kansas City Times, a letter stating that John, myself and he were accused of the robbery. Where he got his authority, I don't know, but one thing I do know, he had none from me. We were not on good terms at the time, nor haven't been for several years. From that time on, mine and John's name has been connected with the James brothers. John hadn't seen either of them for eighteen months before his death. And as for A. C. McCoy, John never saw him in his life. I knew A. C. McCoy during the war, but haven't seen him since, notwithstanding the Appleton City papers say he has been with us in that county for two years. Now, if any respectable man in that county will say he ever saw A. C. McCoy with me or John, I will say no more; or if any respectable man will say that he ever saw any one with us who suited the description of A. C. McCoy, then I will be silent and never more plead innocent.

McCoy is 48 or 49 years old; 6 feet and over in height; dark hair and blue eyes, and low forehead.

Poor John, he has been hunted down and shot like a wild beast, and never was a boy more innocent. But there is a day coming when the secrets of all hearts will be laid open before that All-seeing eye, and every act of our lives will be scrutinized, then will

his skirts be white as the driven snow, while those of his accusers
will be doubly dark.

I will now come to the St. Genevieve robbery. At that time I
was in St. Clair county, Missouri. I do not remember the date, but
Mr. Murphy, one of our neighbors, was sick about that time, and
I sat up with him regularly, where I met with some of the neighbors every day. Dr. L. Lewis was his physician.

As to the Ohio train robbery, I have forgotten the day, I was
also in St. Clair county, Missouri, at that time, and had the pleasure of attending preaching the evening previous to the robbery, at
Monegaw Springs. There were fifty or a hundred persons there
who will testify in any court that I and John were there. I will
give you the names of some of them: Simeon C. Bruce, John S.
Wilson, James Van Allen, Rev. Mr. Smith and lady; Helvin Fickle
and lady, of Greenton Valley, were attending the Springs at that
time, and either of them will testify to the above, for John and I
sat in front of Mr. Smith while he was preaching, and had the
pleasure of his company for a few moments, together with his
lady, and Mr. and Mrs. Fickle, after service. They live at Greenton
Valley, Lafayette county, Missouri, and their evidence would be
taken in the Court of Heaven. As there was no other robbery committed until January, I will come to that time. About the last of
December, 1873, I arrived in Carroll parish, Louisiana. I stayed
there until the 8th of February, 1874. I and brother stayed at
Wm. Dickerson's, near Floyd. Dickerson was Master of a Masonic
Lodge, and during the time the Shreveport stage and the Hot
Springs stage was robbed; also the Gad's Hill robbery. Now, if
the Governor or any one else wants to satisfy himself in regard
to the above he can write to the Masonic Fraternity, Floyd, Carroll parish, Louisiana. I hope the leading journals will investigate
the matter, and then, if they find I have misrepresented anything,
they can show me up to the world as being guilty, but if they find
it as I have stated they surely would have no objections to state
the facts as they are.

You can appeal to the Governor in your own language, and if
he will send men to investigate the above, and is not satisfied of

(*48*)

my innocence, then he can offer the reward for Thos. Coleman Younger, and if he finds me to be innocent, he can make a statement to that effect. I write this hurriedly, and I suppose I have given outlines enough. I want you to take pains and write a long letter for me and sign my name in full.

THOS. COLEMAN YOUNGER.

In order to test the truth of the above letter, so far as the Shreveport stage robbery, the Hot Springs stage robbery, and the Gad's Hill train robbery were concerned, the author of this book wrote to Mr. William Dickerson, of Carroll parish, Louisiana, the gentlemen referred to in the letter. Mr. Dickerson, as we have learned, is a gentleman of standing and respectability in Carroll parish; he was, at the time referred to in Cole Younger's letter, Master of the Masonic Lodge at Floyd, and no hesitancy should be entertained by the reader in placing the utmost confidence in what he says. The following is his reply to our letter, in full, as it was written by Mr. Dickerson, which is also certified to, so far as its truth and correctness are concerned, by ten men of respectability and standing in that community. The letter is as follows:

FLOYD, LA., August 7th, 1875.

MR. A. C. APPLER, Osceola, Mo.:

DEAR SIR—Yours of July 10th was received a few days since. In reply to which I have to state that on the 5th day of December, A. D. 1873, the Younger Brothers arrived at my house, in Carroll parish, La., and remained there until the 8th day of February, A. D. 1874, during which time Cole Younger was engaged in writing the history of Quantrell and his own life. While at my house I asked Cole if he was a Mason, to which he replied in the negative.

Relative to the charges for this information, I will say that it is

(*49*)

worth nothing unless it be a copy of the work you are now preparing to publish, which would be thankfully received. Yours truly, &c.,

WM. DICKERSON.

We, the undersigned citizens of Carroll parish, Louisiana, and neighbors of Mr. William Dickerson, know and believe the statement of his above written regarding the Younger Brothers, to be true and correct.

R. H. GLENN,	T. D. McCAUDLESS,
W. A. CHAPMAN,	W. A. HENDRICK,
A. L. ALLEY,	I. L. CHEATHAM,
CHAS. H. WEBB,	O. HERRINGTON,
I. S. HERRING.	R. I. LONDON.

THE GENEVIEVE BANK ROBBERY.

I hereby certify that I attended Mr. Murphy, of St. Clair county, Missouri, during his sickness in November, 1872, and that on the day the St. Genevieve, Missouri, Bank was said to have been robbed, I saw at the house of Mr. Murphy, in the county of St. Clair, Thomas Coleman Younger, generally called Cole Younger, and that he could not possibly have had any hand in said bank robbery, as he was sitting up with and nursing Murphy during his sickness.

L. LEWIS, M. D.,
Treasurer and Collector of St. Clair County, Mo.

THE IOWA TRAIN ROBBERY.

We, whose names are hereto subscribed, certify that we saw Thomas Coleman Younger at Monegaw Springs, St. Clair county, Missouri, on Sunday, July 20th, 1873, the day previous to the Iowa Train Robbery, which occurred on Monday morning, July 21st, 1873, and that said Thomas Coleman Younger could not possibly have had any hand in said robbery.

SIMEON E. BRUCE,
JAMES VAN ALLEN,
PARSON SMITH,
ROBERT WHITE.

(50)

Cole Younger with Quantrell.

The Flannery Fight

Thomas Coleman Younger, commonly called Cole Younger, joined the forces of Quantrell, at that time comprising only eight men, about the first of January, 1862. They were then camped on the Little Blue, in Jackson county, Missouri. All of the men comprising this little band, were young men of standing and respectability in that community, and some of them were sons of the most wealthy and prominent citizens of the county. Very early in the spring Quantrell and his little band of nine men crossed over into Kansas to see if they could not recover some of the fine blooded horses stolen from Henry W. Younger the year previous. After searching around a day or two without discovering the whereabouts of any of the stock, they returned to Missouri, stopping for the night at the house of a friend, Flannery, in Jackson county, Missouri. As it afterwards proved, they were followed by a Capt. Peabody, with one hundred men, who surrounded the house at which they were stopping. After tapping on the door to awake the inmates, Capt. Peabody demanded of Quantrell an unconditional surrender. Quantrell replied that he would give him an answer in ten minutes, which was allowed him. During the

Cole Younger

ten minutes time allowed him, Quantrell arranged his men in different parts of the house, the better to enable them to fire with effect, as also to be protected from the fire of the enemy. Cole Younger was placed in the loft, at an attic window, while the other men were stationed at the doors and windows. When all necessary arrangements had been made, Quantrell stepped to the door and told Peabody that he would not surrender, accompanying his words with a round from his double-barrel shotgun, which killed the First Lieutenant under Peabody. All of Quantrell's men followed, pouring a deadly fire into the ranks of the enemy. The Jayhawkers immediately returned the fire, and the fight was kept up for about two hours, when the ell of the house was discovered to be on fire. Cole Younger was then called down stairs and preparations made to charge the enemy and escape. After making a careful examination of the situation of affairs, Quantrell concluded it was not possible to escape. It was then concluded to keep up a steady fire on the enemy in front of the house, hoping to compel them to give way. This plan was tried for some time without the desired effect. By this time the fire had so far progressed that a portion of the roof of the main house was beginning to fall in. Quantrell then determined to try strategy, and, gathering his men about him, to give them instructions, found two men missing and one wounded. Cole Younger searched the house and found the two missing men under the bed, and told them to come out, as the house was on fire and they would be burned up alive if they did not try to escape with the rest. They did not come out and were burned to death. Quantrell then explained his plan to his men, which was to take

(53)

pillows, place hats on them, and stick them out of the windows, hoping thereby to draw the fire of the enemy, and while their guns were empty make a charge on them and escape, firing as they rushed from the house. This strategetic movement was carried out and succeeded very well, and as soon as the most of them were supposed to have emptied their guns, Quantrell threw open the door and ordered his men to follow him, rushing out of the house and emptying the contents of their guns among the enemy, which caused them to give way, while they rushed through their line. In their flight they met with an obstacle in the way of a picket fence, which caused them to scatter some. The Jayhawkers, knowing the obstruction that was in their way, closed in behind them. Cole Younger became entirely separated from the others, and after scaling the fence, was followed by some cavalry, who were stationed in the field. He made the best possible time across the field, and when the cavalry would approach within shooting range of him, he would halt and present his gun, as though about to fire, when they would throw themselves on the opposite side of their horses and halt. He would then take the advantage of this and continue his flight, and when they would near him again, he would resort to the same strategy, with the same effect. This was repeated several times, until at length he reached the fence and brush, when he made good his escape, not however, until he had wounded one man and killed another of his pursuers. Quantrell and the rest of the men also made their escape. In the fight fifteen of the Jayhawkers were killed and a number wounded. All of Quantrell's men lost their horses.

Cole Younger rejoined Quantrell in a day or two. Their future operations were then discussed, and in view of the fact that they had been slipped up on, in the last engagement, retaliation in like manner was determined on. While thus planning and arranging for future operations, the Federals stationed at Harrisonville and Independence were not idle, well knowing that they had a wily foe to contend with, although few in number. Knowing that they had dismounted Quantrell and his men, and supposing most of them wounded, they at once concluded that the wounded would fall an easy prey to their untiring energy, and at once determined to scour the country thoroughly, and force the citizens to give them information of their whereabouts. Old men were imprisoned, young men murdered outright, and the women insulted and abused, with the view of gaining information of the whereabouts of Quantrell and his men. All this failed them. In the mean time, Quantrell, learning these facts, succeeded in mounting his men and started on the war trail, having the assurance of the citizens that his movements would be kept secret. They were constantly on the alert, and on Friday morning, two weeks after the engagement at Flannery's, Quantrell received information through Union men, that the Federal Colonel stationed at Independence had learned that Cole Younger had stopped for a day or two at old man Blythe's, and had determined to send out a scouting party to Blythe's house, with full authority to force the old gentleman to reveal the whereabouts of Younger. Quantrell, knowing Blythe to be a particular friend of Younger's, asked Younger what they had better do. Younger replied: "They better not hurt that old man." After further consultation it was agreed that Blythe should be notified of the fact, and told to secrete himself that day, while Quantrell and his men would watch their movements, and, if possible, prevent them from reaching Blythe's house, on the Harrisonville and Independence road. As soon as possible Quantrell stationed his men at the Cut, which is about thirty feet deep, one hundred and fifty yards in length, and quite narrow at the bottom. But the Federals, by some means, were thrown off their direct course and did not come that way. After waiting there until late in the afternoon, Quantrell proposed to Younger to ride down the road towards Blythe's house, which was about three miles distant, and see if he could hear anything of them. After traveling out on the road about one mile he met an old negro man belonging to Mr. Moore, who seemed to be very much frightened. After being questioned he told Younger the Federals had been at Blythe's house, and failing to find the old gentleman at home, proceeded to reap vengeance upon his son, a lad of about twelve years of age.

Killing of Young Blythe.

Young Blythe was taken to the barn and told that he must tell where Quantrell and his men were, or else they would kill him. The boy parlied with them a few moments, watched an opportunity, and then broke and run to the house, entering the door in the midst of a perfect shower of bullets fired at him from the barn. The boy then got an old pistol that was in the house and passed out at the back door, thinking to make his escape. While getting over the fence in the rear of the house he was observed and

The Attack on Flannery's House

fired on, one shot striking him in the back, when he fell to the ground. The Jayhawkers then closed in on him to finish their work, when the boy, hearing them coming towards him, and knowing they would kill him, turned over on his side, resting on his elbow, and when they neared him fired two shots, killing one man and mortally wounding the second. They then made short work of him, riddling his body with bullets. The old negro was there on an errand and witnessed the whole proceeding. After the boy had been killed the negro became frightened and left, not knowing but what it would be his turn next. He took to the brush, and after traveling some distance got out on the main road, where he met Cole Younger and related to him the killing of young Blythe. Younger then asked the negro what direction they had taken, but he was unable to tell him, having left the place before they started.

The Fight at the Blue Cut.

Cole Younger then rode down the road a short distance, to an eminence, which commanded a good view of the road for some distance, when he saw the Federals coming. Riding back hastily until he overtook the negro, he told him to go down to the Blue Cut and tell Mr. Heller, with whom he was acquainted, to look out, and he would report to him soon. Younger again rode back to the eminence, where he could plainly see the Federals coming up the road from the South, directly approaching the Blue Cut. He then put spurs to his horse and rode back to where Quantrell was, telling him what had happened, and that they were coming up the road. Quantrell then dismounted his men and arranged them on both sides of the

Cut, on top, as well as at each end, with instructions to let the Federals pass in and then close up and fire on them. There were about thirty of the Jayhawkers. They marched on up the road and entered the Cut, not suspecting danger, until the rear men closed in on them and fired. As soon as the men stationed in the rear opened fire, those on top followed, pouring a deadly volley into their confused ranks, which was followed by those stationed in front, closing in and opening fire on them. Having been taken completely by surprise, they knew not which way to turn or what to do, while Quantrell's men continued to pour volley after volley into their ranks, which were by this time being thinned; men and horses were killed, wounded and dying, and the shrieks of the wounded were heard above the din of musketry, from one end of the Cut to the other. About twenty of the Jayhawkers were killed, but few escaping. None of Quantrell's men were hurt. As one of the Jayhawkers dashed out in front of the Cut, Cole Younger grabbed his horse by the bridle, and after checking his speed, drew his revolver and shot the rider dead.

The Indian Creek Fight.

Shortly after the preceeding occurrence, while Quantrell and his nine men were camped on Indian Creek, in Jackson county, Missouri, the Jayhawkers stationed at Independence took their whole force and surrounded the timber and brush in which Quantrell and his men were camped, twenty-five or thirty acres, having with them two pieces of artillery. After they had surrounded the camp the artillery was stationed in a lane running down to the timber, and they threw shells pretty lively for awhile, the cavalry having been stationed on the opposite side, in an open field, where it was supposed Quantrell's men would come out to make their escape. This occurred shortly before night. Quantrell, seeing the predicament in which he was placed, secreted his men in a ravine, which protected them from the artillery, and at the same time afforded them an opportunity to keep up a fire on the cavalry whenever they made their appearance in a certain direction, within range of their guns. The fight was kept up until dark, when the Federal officer threw a strong guard around the entire camp, to prevent the possibility of their escape. During the night, as was afterwards ascertained, a large number of the Federals were dismounted and drilled as infantry, preparatory to a charge upon the camp in the morning, thus hoping to capture or kill all of the Guerrillas. While all this was going on, on the one side, Quantrell was devising ways and means of escape. While Quantrell and Haller were thus planning, Haller suggested that Cole Younger had better be called in the council, as he knew every inch of the country, and was a perfect backwoodsman. When Younger was called, he gave a detailed account of the location, &c. There was a farmhouse and barn inside of the Federal lines, and also quite a large lot of stock. Younger at length suggested that they stampede the stock, to draw the fire of the enemy, as well as create confusion in their ranks, and thus, while in confusion, make their escape. The stock was at length stampeded and driven through the Federal lines, many of them being killed and wounded. The stampede created much confusion in the Federal ranks, causing quite a gap to be opened, through which Quantrell and his men passed out.

The Federals did not discover their mistake for some time, as the night was dark. Cole Younger led the way, and when near the pickets, they took advantage of a stone fence by crawling on their hands and knees, single file, making good their escape. After they had safely passed all danger, Quantrell, in talking over the matter, expressed dissatisfaction at the result or termination of it, and having, as he believed, a thorough knowledge of the position of the Federals, and knowing that but a small force was left with the artillery, in the rear, determined that he would, if possible, gain possession of it in the morning, by taking them by surprise. Younger was then consulted as to the best means of gaining a favorable position to observe the movements of the Federals in the morning, so as to be ready and in position to charge the artillery at the opportune moment. It was then agreed that the men should be fed and refreshed for the morning service, while Younger would go out and gain knowledge of the true position of the Federals. This he accomplished by stealthily crawling around until he came near to them. He soon found out that they had not materially changed their position. At times he was actually right among them. After fully satisfying himself of these facts, and also ascertaining that a large force had been dismounted, and their horses placed in charge of a small negro guard, he returned to Quantrell and detailed to him the information he had obtained.

Quantrell at once determined to charge the artillery in the morning, capture it, and then open fire on the infantry, at the same time putting in a few random shots among the guards with horses. At four o'clock in the morning Quantrell's forces were in line, with Cole Younger in front, as guide, with instructions to lead them to some practicable point of attack near the artillerymen. This was successfully done by leading them in a circuitous route to an old orchard, which was full of volunteer hemp, the better enabling them to gain a favorable position. Finally, they were stationed within forty yards of the artillery. One man was then placed where the movements of the cavalry and infantry could be observed in the morning. When daylight arrived Quantrell received information from the man on the lookout, that the infantry were preparing to make a charge through the brush, while the cavalry were posted on the opposite side (where it was supposed Quantrell and his men would come out in trying to make their escape.)

About this time a heavy force of cavalry was seen approaching from the East, who were supposed to be, by the Federals, Col. Up. Hays' Confederates, as they were expected daily about that time. Each party observed the other about the same time. The Federal cavalry at once passed around the timber to the infantry, with the view of consolidating their forces. The officer in command of the infantry, seeing the movement of the cavalry, then ordered his men to fall back to their horses, so they could quickly mount in case it was necessary. The Federals, in their surmises that the approaching cavalry was that of Col. Up. Hays' command, were mistaken, as it afterwards turned out to be Jennison and his band of Kansas red-legs. After this movement of the Federals, Quantrell became satisfied that they had abandoned their idea of capturing him and his men, and were looking out for their own safety. In the meanwhile Quantrell took in the situation at a glance, and sprang like a tiger upon the cavalrymen, engaging them in a hand to hand fight, killing all who did not immediately take to a cornfield near by. Having thus secured the two guns in a moment, George Todd, one of Quantrell's best men, and who, by the way, was an old artilleryman, took charge of the guns and at once opened a severe fire on the infantry, who were then coming up the lane to gain their horses, while an occasional shot was thrown in among the horses, effectually stampeding the guard. After the guard with the horses was stampeded, a most terrific fire was kept up on the infantry, who, by this time, were retreating in the direction of Little Santa Fe.

This little brush completely demoralized Jennison also, who thought the rebs were about in great numbers, and he also made a hasty retreat in the direction of Kansas, throwing away every description of plunder, which he had been gathering up as he passed through the country. Thus the reader will observe that two armies of Federals, with artillery, were frightened,—first, by one another; and secondly, by nine of Quantrell's men—their artillery captured, and they driven from the field. This is no fancy sketch, but a stubborn fact, and one which, when the facts in the case became known, created considerable talk and laughter throughout that section of the country. Quantrell then tok the artillery and threw it into the Big Blue, and mounted his men on the best horses that were captured from the Federals.

After this little affair became known the Federal authorities at Kansas City sent for Jennison and his band of Kansas Red Legs, and an indiscriminate slaughter was carried on throughout that whole country by Jennison and his men, assisted some by others, while the Federal forces stationed at Kansas City, Independence, &c., held the posts. Such was the conduct of the Federal forces throughout this section of the State, that nearly every man of nerve and pluck at once rallied to the support of Quantrell, until his little band of nine men soon increased to the number of sixty, which enabled him to do better and more effective service. Skirmishing was an almost everyday occurrence, and during that summer hundreds of the Jayhawkers were sent to other homes than that of Kansas.

Quantrell Organizes a Company.

Quantrell then proceeded to organize a company, in regular military order, he being elected Captain. Wm. Haller was elected First Lieutenant; Cole Younger Second Lieutenant, and George Todd, Third Lieutenant. Having thus effected a complete organization, Quantrell at once commenced to shadow the operations of the Federal forces, keeping spies continually in Kansas City and Independence. There was scarely a man or woman in that whole community but what constituted himself and herself a committee of one to watch the operations of the Jayhawkers and give Quantrell information. Even some strong Union men acted as spies, so utterly disgusted were the citizens with the conduct of the Federals, who were carrying on an indiscriminate murder and robbery. Quantrell and his men committed none of these depredations, but on the contrary, endeavored by every possible means to prevent them being perpetrated. To this circumstance may be attributed the fact of Union men giving information to Quantrell.

(64)

So complete and thorough was the co-operation of the citizens with Quantrell, that the slightest demonstration on the part of the Federal forces was duly noted and immediately reported to him. Not a scout could leave town or approach from Kansas, without his knowing the fact and operations set on foot to check the movement. Quantrell kept his men divided into four squads, the better and more effectually to execute his work. One squad was placed under the charge of Cole Younger, one under George Todd, one under Haller, and the other Quantrell had under his immediate control; the whole force concentrating whenever deemed necessary. Quantrell always carried with him an Opelousas or Texas steer's horn, which had a peculiar sound, and could be heard at a distance of about four miles. All of his men were acquainted with its peculiar sound, and whenever a certain blast from it was given, all hands rallied to the assistance of their commander. Another peculiar feature of the sounding of this horn was, that with it he was able to make his officers understand what he desired them to do, all having been drilled to certain signals. As before remarked, scarcely a day passed without some skirmishing, and in almost every instance the Jayhawkers suffered in loss of men.

Two Men Killed and One Captured.

In June, 1862, while the Jayhawkers were watching a ford on the Little Blue, three of Quantrell's men rode into the river to water their horses, when they were fired upon from ambush, two being killed and the third wounded and captured. The wounded man was taken to Independence, where he was placed in jail and abused in the most shameful manner. On learning of his treatment, Quantrell determined to release him as soon as his wounds were sufficiently healed to enable him to travel. He then set all of his men on the alert to capture some of the Federals, to be held for exchange, and for the good treatment of the prisoner held at Independence. No opportunity presented itself for several weeks.

Two Successful Sorties

At length Quantrell learned that the prisoner held at Independence was to be hung at the court house on a certain day. He at once determined on a plan to capture some of the Jayhawkers. Haller, with four men, was sent into Independence at night, to the house of his (Haller's) mother, to gain information in regard to the position of the Federal pickets. They all arrived safely, and there learned from an old servant that four of the pickets had been stationed at an old woolen mill south of town. Haller, knowing the ground to be very rough in that vicinity, concluded to make a personal reconnoisance of the position, in order to gain knowledge of their exact location. He then left the men at the house of his mother, and proceeded on foot to make the examination. Finding it practicable, he at once determined to kill or capture the pickets, but decided not to kill them if possible to capture them. Returning to the house, he there learned that a picket force was stationed on the opposite side of the town, and knowing that if he made an attack upon the pickets at the woolen mill, the Federal forces would be rapidly thrown in that direction, and thus prevent him making his escape with the prisoners; and knowing that Cole Younger was stationed at the old Younger farm, three miles south of town, he sent a runner to him with instructions to make a spirited demonstration on the river road, to enable Haller to capture the pickets at the woolen mill.

Younger at once mounted his men and proceeded to do as directed. After passing around the town he took steps to ascertain the exact position of the pickets on that road, and finding they were stationed near Hiram Young's factory, he cautiously approached the rear end of the building, dismounted his men, opened the door, and all led their horses through the building to the front door, which opened out into the street between the pickets and the main camp. The building was a large one-story frame, used for a wagon factory, without flooring. Younger then mounted his men and rode noiselessly down the street, when he saw at a glance that the pickets had not suspected his approach. Two of them were sitting on an old bridge, while the rest were sleeping near by. Quick as thought, Younger and his men dashed down the street on the pickets, yelling at the top of their voices, and firing as they neared them. The two pickets that were awake returned the fire, wounding one of Younger's men and killing one horse. One of them was captured but the other got away. Those who were asleep jumped up and ran away, when they were fired on, two being killed and four captured. Younger then took his prisoners and passed around the town, driving in the pickets on the Blue Hill road, and then made his way to Quantrell's camp.

As soon as Haller heard the firing of Younger's men he jumped his pickets, captured them without firing a gun, and straightway went to Quantrell's camp with his prisoners.

After Younger and Haller reported with their prisoners, Quantrell wrote a letter to the Federal officer at Independence, stating that if he killed the wounded prisoner he held, the prisoners in his hands would share a similar fate; but that if he released him, as also the old men he held, some 20, he, Quantrell, would release the prisoners he held on parole. The Federal officer finally acceded to the proposition and both sides released their prisoners. When Quantrel released his prisoners, there was among them an Irishman who refused to return with his companions, but insisted on joining the forces of Quantrell, at the same time stating that he had, for some time, been desirous of joining his company, and determined to do so at the first favorable opportunity, and now that an opportunity presented itself, he was going to carry out his intention, which he did.

Younger Shoots His Cousin

One night Cole Younger went to the house of his grand-mother, Mrs. Fristo, where he stayed for supper, hitching his horse back of the house, in the brush. After eating supper and talking to the old lady for some time, Cole concluded he would return to camp. He bid the old lady good-bye, and walked out on the porch, which was elevated some four feet from the ground and open underneath. The moon was shining brightly at the time. Just as he was about to step off the porch he was surprised to meet his cousin, Capt. Charles Younger, of the State Militia. Both recognized each other and shook hands. After shaking

hands Capt. Younger said: "You are my prisoner." Cole
scanned him closely for a moment, and then, quick as
lightning, grabbed his revolver, threw it into his face and
fired, Capt. Younger dropping dead, as Cole supposed,
when he, Cole, sprang from the porch and ran up through
the yard, as he then discovered that the house was surrounded by soldiers. When near the fence and brush,
where his horse was, Cole fell over a bee-gum and dislo-
cated his knee; at this very instant a shower of lead passed
over him, cutting the back of his coat into ribbons, but
not drawing blood. Had he not fallen the very instant he
did, he would have been instantly killed. With his knee
badly injured, Cole crawled to the brush, got on his horse
and made his escape.

The Federal Major Linden.

There was a Major Linden, of the 7th Missouri Cavalry,
Volunteers, stationed at Harrisonville, who did not ap-
prove of the course pursued by the Jayhawkers, as well as
some of the Federal officers. His idea of conducting the
war was to make friends of those who differed with him,
and, instead of driving men into the Southern army by
ill-treatment, he endeavored, by good treatment, to induce
those who were in to forsake the cause in which they had
enlisted. He would not allow any of his men to commit
depredations or take anything without paying for it. The
course he pursued made everybody respect him who was
disposed to see the unhappy state of affairs that existed in
the country brought to a speedy termination, while the
Jayhawkers and all evil-disposed persons denounced his
course. He denounced and punished Union men and

Rebels alike, whenever they did wrong. In one sense it might be said he acted in concert with Quantrell. One day, while Neugent's Jayhawkers were prowling through the country they took as prisoner Richard DeJarnett, a highly respected citizen, taking him to Harrisonville and handing him over to Maj. Linden, preferring charges against him of stealing and various other depredations. Linden tried him and found that none of the charges preferred against him could be sustained, when he turned him loose. This made Neugent quite angry, and he threatened to do wonders. Linder paid but little attention to him for a while, until finally he gave him to understand that if he, Neugent, did not conduct himself properly, he would take him in hands and punish him as he deserved. Linden, being unwilling to carry on a warfare as practiced by most of the Federal officers, became disgusted and resigned in September, 1862.

Capture of Mail, Ammunition, Etc.

A citizen of Harrisonville frequently carried the mail to Lexington, and one day Quantrell learned that this citizen had gone to Lexington to bring the mail, a lot of ammunition, some uniforms, etc., when he at once determined to capture the whole outfit, and requested Cole Younger to do up the job. Cole soon started on the errand and brought back the whole concern. There was quite a lot of ammunition, a Colonel and Lieutenant Colonel's uniform, the mail, etc. The prisoner was turned loose. None of Quantrell's officers would put on the uniforms, much less wear them, and the men would frequently put them on some one and get them to strut about the camp, giving orders, etc., which would create much merriment.

As soon as it became known to the Federal authorities that the mail, ammunition, etc., had been captured, scouting parties were sent out in every direction to recapture the lost property, but without avail. The only good accomplished was the loss of some of the Jayhawkers.

Quantrell Makes Bold Strikes.

Quantrell, now having sixty-three men, all well armed, mounted and drilled for effective service, decided to make some bold strokes. He concentrated his forces at Lee's Summit, in Jackson county, Missouri, keeping the main body of his men together, secreted, while Cole Younger was detailed to make violent demonstrations on the Federal camps at Harrisonville, Independence and Kansas City alternating between the different places. Younger and his squad of six men, were to draw the Federals out of town, to the place where Quantrell and his men were secreted, and by this means they would be able to do much execution. While thus engaged, Younger would frequently ride within shooting distance of the Federal pickets at Independence, fire upon them, and then retreat, hoping to induce them to follow him. But the Federals had learned what kind of men they had to deal with, and seldom followed any distance. Federal communication between Harrisonville and Independence was entirely cut off, except an occasional mail that was sent out under a strong guard.

Another Fight at the Blue Cut.

One day Quantrell learned that the mail would pass, by the way of Pleasant Hill, from Harrisonville to Independence, under a strong guard of Neugent's men. He at once determined to give them a round. Younger was detailed to attend to them, whose force of six men, by this time, had increased considerably, by the addition of new recruits. He at once placed spies all along the road, to watch the movements of the Jayhawkers. At length he received information that they were taking the Blue Cut road, He at once proceeded to arrange his men in a similar manner as did Quantrell on a previous occasion, at this same place, heretofore mentioned. After arranging his men another runner arrived with the intelligence that the party was commanded by Capt. Long, an old acquaintance of Younger. He was also told that Isaac Shoat, a deserter from Quantrell, and a man by the name of Coon, a notorious house-burner, were in the party. Younger then went to every one of his men, gave them a minute description of Capt. Long, and told them by no means to shoot at him.

It was natural to suppose that the Federals would be on their guard when passing through the Cut, after being previously trapped there, but such awas not the case. It was apparent that the men had been drinking freely of ardent spirits, and seemed not to think or care of consequences. As they approached the Cut one of them was heard to remark: "What if that damn Quantrell was here again?" His companion replied: "Oh, I guess he has gone South—there is only a small squad here under Cole Younger, now." By this time they were about midway of the Cut, Capt. Long riding behind, when Cole Younger sprang upon a rock commanding the position, and, in a loud voice, demanded their surrender. His summons to surrender was answered by a volley of musketry, when a murderous fire was opened upon them by the Guerrillas from behind rocks, trees and logs. The Jayhawkers kept up quite a spirited resistance for awhile, Capt. Long shouting to his men to stand their ground, until they were mowed down to such an extent that it was found necessary for them to retreat, if any of them expected to escape. Just at this moment Younger's men closed in at the head and foot of the cut, and as Younger entered the road Capt. Long and the deserter, Shoat, dashed by. Younger shot Capt. Long's horse from under him, the horse falling upon him and pinioning him to the ground; when Younger fired at Shoat, who, by this time, was fifty yards off, shooting him as he supposed, in the back. Younger than sprang to Capt. Long's assistance, rolling the horse off of him, and raising him up, asked him if he was hurt. "No, nothing more than a bruised leg." Younger then told him to sit down, and he would go down the cut and see what had become of the other boys. When he reached the top of the hill, where he could see down into the cut, his eyes beheld a confused mass of men and horses, horses lying upon riders and riders lying upon horses, dead, wounded and dying, while those of the Federals who had escaped unhurt, surrendered unconditionally. Younger ordered the prisoners to march up the hill to where Capt. Long was sitting, and after placing them under guard, he turned to Capt. Long, saying, "Come, Al., let us go down and see who is hurt." While looking around through the confused mass of men and horses, Younger discovered the notorious Coon, wounded in the back part of the thigh. Coon immediately recognized Younger, and begged him to spare his life.

Younger replied, "You cowardly dog, you deserve to die right here, but you need not be alarmed, it is not my style to hurt a man when he is down." Younger then called for assistance, and the wounded were carried to a creek, near by, given water, their wounds dressed, etc. After all had been cared for as well as could be, Younger turned to Capt. Long and said: "I guess the wounded can now get along without my assistance, as I must be going." Long then asked: "What are you going to do with me?" Younger replied: "Haven't we always been friends?" "Yes, replied Long." "I never go back on a friend," replied Younger, "and hope we will always have reason to look upon each other as friends. Now, Al., take care of your wounded, and do the best you can. I will leave you here." As Younger turned to go away he remarked, "the very man I wanted, that deserter, Shoat, has made his escape." Younger then rode back to where the prisoners were under guard, and, after making them a speech, advising them to go home and stay there, released them. Forming his men into line, he turned to ride away, when he got a glimpse of somebody coming towards him on horseback, and, thinking him to be a runner with some valuable information, waited until he arrived. The rider, after being interrogated, informed Younger that he was going for a doctor. Younger asked, "Who for?" He replied, "There is a man up at the house of Dr. Nolan's badly wounded, who fell off his horse when directly opposite the house." Younger then asked his name, but the man did not recollect it. Some one of the men asked if it was Shoat, when he replied, "Yes, that's it it." Some of the boys proposed that they go up there and finish him, when Younger replied there was no use in that, it was not his style of doing business. The Doctor was procured, but only arrived there to find that his wound was mortal and that he was then dying. Before breathing his last he told the Doctor that he tried to make his escape, as when he saw Younger he knew he would be killed, and felt confident Younger had shot him. Younger then told his men to scatter and meet him at Quantrell's camp.

This engagement was immortalized by a little ditty, composed by a friend of Younger's, sung to the time and chorus of Dixie, one verse of which is as follows:

> "As we were crossing Little Blue,
> We met Younger and his crew;
> They killed Cap's horse and robbed the mail,
> And shot our Coon through the tail."

The Walnut Creek Fight.

In July, 1862, immediately following the second engagement of the Little Blue, the Federals, with forces numbering about 2,000 men, were continually scouting around through the Sny and Blue Hills, hunting Quantrell and his little band. Skirmishing was an every day occurrence. At length Quantrell, seeing that their whole force was kept in Jackson county, determined to give them the dodge and strike Harrisonville, Cass county, in their rear. Mounting his men, he slipped out of the Sny Hills under cover of night, and made his way direct for Harrisonville, about twenty miles distant. He reached within a mile of Harrisonville just as day broke in the morning, when, looking back on the road, he discovered that he was closely pursued by a large force of Federals. He then changed his

plan of operations and took the road for Austin, hoping to
fall in upon a Federal camp. When he reached Austin he
found the place evacuated, the camp fire still burning. He
then dismounted, fed the horses, the men ate their breakfast, and when about to start the Federals were again discovered coming up the road some six hundred strong.
Quantrell turned to Haller and said, "All the Feds. in the
country are on our trail, and this is a strange country to
me. It would be best for us to make our way back to the
Blue Hills, where, if they press us too hard, we can
scatter and throw them off our trail, and then concentrate
our forces and attack them in their rear." Haller replied,
"But who knows the country; we cannot go back direct,
but must take a circuitous route." Quantrell then replied,
"I will see Younger; he will be more likely to know the
country than any one else." Younger was then asked if he
could lead them back to the Blue Hills, and he replied
that he could, as he was perfectly familiar with the country. Younger then took the lead, going out the Dayton road,
and when he reached Dayton there learned that the Rider
Boys, of bushwacking notoriety, were at home. He then
passed on to Mrs. Rider's house, where he met John Rider,
who had twelve men under his command. Younger then
related to Rider the situation of things, telling him they
had use for every man they could possibly raise. Rider
asked Quantrell how he was going to get out of that scrape,
as the Federals could then be seen approaching. Quantrell
replied, "I am leaving the matter with my White Haired
Boy," a name he often gave Cole Younger. "Well," replied Rider, "he knows every hog path, and can carry you
through safe." Younger then asked Rider if he would join

them, telling him he had heard of some of his exploits. Rider answered in the affirmative, saying, "I am always in for a little fun." The forces were then swelled to seventy-five men.

They then took the road to Walnut Creek, in Johnson county, the Federals pressing them closely. After reaching Walnut Creek, they took the brush and the Federals lost their trail. After travelling through the brush some distance they entered the main road, north, and travelled direct to the Sny Hills. After marching some six miles on the road, they stopped to feed and get dinner, having dismounted in an old orchard, back of the house. While busy feeding their horses and grooming, the pickets came in and reported that the Federals were coming in on their trail, from the South, 200 strong.

The Federals approached within about half a mile of the house, when they observed that something was wrong there, and at once halted and formed in line of battle. Finally they concluded to send out an advance of twelve men, to ascertain definitely there were any Guerrillas about the premises. Quantrell, in the mean time, had fallen back and taken a position so that he could make an effectual resistance. He fell back to a small tract of timber, with a steep bluff on each side, where he felled trees, wrapped grape vines from tree to tree, and thus made his place of defence wholly unapproachable by cavalry, leaving but a small opening for Younger and his men to pass in, when compelled to retreat.

Younger was left with a squad of but twelve men, with instructions to do the best he could, and gradually retreat to where Quantrell and his main force was stationed. Finally,

(77)

the Federal advance of twelve men started in the direction of the house, and when Younger saw that they were advancing, resorted to strategy, by getting the lady of the house to take their blankets and hang them over the fence, as though she had been washing, while Younger and his men crawled up behind the fence unobserved, and prepared for their approach, as soon as they came within range. The plan hit upon proved a complete success, and when the Federal advance rode up within close range, Younger and his men rose up from behind the fence and poured a deadly fire into them, killing all but one man. This was done in plain view of the Federal line, and they, perceiving the wholesale slaughter of their men, at once commenced making preparations for a retreat. Just as they were about to retrace their steps, they were reinforced by 200 men from Butler. As soon as the reinforcements arrived they resolved to avenge the death of their companions, and made a charge upon the house. Younger then slowly retreated in the direction of Quantrell's barricade, occasionally sending back a volley at his pursuers. Quantrell met him in the edge of the timber and showed him the way to enter, and as soon as he entered the fortifications the entrance was closed by felling trees, which had previously been prepared, so that a few strokes of the axe would bring them down. Quantrell had all of his men dismounted, their horses secured back in the ravine, out of the way of the bullets, and the men ready to open fire as soon as the enemy approached within range of their double-barrel shot-guns. Scarcely had Younger and his men entered the enclosure and dismounted, ere the Federals made a charge upon the works. The first charge only resulted in

(78)

heavy loss to their cavalry, and they soon retreated a short distance. Quantrell always carried with him a wagon-load of Sharp's rifles to be used for long range, and these deadly weapons were now brought into requisition, and soon caused the Federals to retreat still further back.

Four separate and distinct charges were made by the Federals, each time resulting as the first. They were then reinforced by about 200 more men, and the fifth and sixth charges were made, resulting as before. Quantrell then concluded, although the odds were largely against him, to mount his men and charge the enemy upon the open field. After he had opened a path sufficient to allow of an exit from his work, mounted his men and got outside of the barricade, he observed that the Federals were again being largely reinforced, when he determined to abandon the charge. The Federals, observing Quantrell's movement, again made a charge, this time endeavoring to force an entrance where Quantrell and his men had entered, but they were met with such a deadly fire that they were compelled to retreat.

It was now near night, and Quantrell commenced felling trees and showing signs of strengthening his position, which led the enemy to believe that he meant to stay there. This seemed to satisfy them, and they were left to plan their operations for the next morning, while Quantrell and his men slipped out down the ravine.

During the last charge on his works, while Quantrell had his men mounted, his horse was shot from under him, and he received a shot in the right knee. Several other horses belonging to the men of his command were killed. Quantrell rode behind Younger, while the other men who were dismounted rode behind their comrades. They finally made their way to the Sny Hills, where they divided up into small squads and thus effectually eluded their pursuers.

Trial of an Enfield Rifle.

Upon one occasion Quantrell's band encountered a party of Jayhawkers numbering thirty or more. A dozen of the Jayhawkers were killed and fifteen captured. They were taken to camp and the question of their fate soon settled. After supper, and while the shades of evening were approaching, Cole Younger got out an Enfield rifle captured that day. It was the first he had ever seen, and its merits and demerits were discussed by the men. Opinions differed as to its superior qualities. One of the men remarked that he heard it would kill at the distance of a mile. Younger replied, "if that is so, the force of the discharge must be terrific." Another banteringly remarked, if the new gun would kill at a mile distant, a ball, at a short range, would go through ten men. Younger raised up from the saddle upon which he had been sitting and remarked, that is easy to demonstrate. When the prisoners heard this remark they felt sure their time had come. The fifteen prisoners were then placed in a line, one behind the other, and Cole Younger took the gun, played with the lock a moment, to "get the hang of it," and then measured off fifteen paces in front of the line formed, wheeled about, looked calmly and soberly into the faces of the doomed men, and then fired. The first, second and third man dropped lifeless, without a groan. Muttering a contemptuous condemnation of the new rifle, Younger, without moving from his tracks, continued his experiments. Seven times the rifle was discharged, each time the Guerrillas commenting carelessly upon the merits of the Enfield, and fifteen of the Jayhawkers lay in an inanimate heap upon the grass.

A Sharp Little Fight.

In the summer of 1862, Cole Younger and six of his companions in arms, watched a house of bad repute in Jackson county, where the Federal soldiers were in the habit of visiting, to catch some of the red legs and Jayhawkers, who, he learned, were there almost nightly. One evening about dusk he and his party made a charge upon the house. Four of his men, however, failed to charge with him. There were six men in the house at the time, and three of them immediately retreated out of the back doors and windows. The other three stood their ground and made a desperate fight, one shot of the first round killing a comrade of Cole Younger. Cole Younger fired two shots in rapid succession, both of which told with deadly effect. As Cole was about to dismount and rush into the house, the third man fired at him from the upper door with a double-barrel shot gun, loaded with buckshot, some of the shot entering his body under the right shoulder. He carries some of the lead to this day. He then fell from his horse, but immediately after rose up and rushed into the house, where he found the third man about to escape out of the back door, when he fired at him and brought him down. As soon as the fighting commenced the women made their escape from the house. Cole then sank to the floor from the loss of blood. As soon as he recovered he called

(*81*)

his comrades to come to his assistance, which they did, and helped him on his horse. The party then rode fifty miles before Cole stopped to have his wounds dressed, and receive medical treatment.

A Brush with Jayhawkers.

In June, 1862, while with Quantrell in Cass county, Missouri, Cole Younger and a few men stopped at the house of a friend to get dinner, near Harrisonville, a sentinel being stationed near the house while the rest dined. Scarcely had they commenced to eat, before the guard gave the alarm that a squad of Federals was approaching the house, by the lane. This lane was two miles in length, running to the town of Harrisonville. Fifteen of Quantrell's men were at the other end of the lane, a few hundred yards distant, where another lane crosses, and in the rear of the field was brush. All along this lane lay grain-fields, which the sunny days of June had turned into waving gold. Nature seemed to smile all over these beautiful rolling farms, and say to the hungry soldier, "in a few weeks I will feed you." But alas, all was doomed to be destroyed before nature had fulfilled the promise.

Cole Younger, who was acting Captain of the scout, ordered his men to mount their horses and make for the timber, at the mouth of the lane. At the head of this lane was another lane leading off to the South. The main road leading to town came in from the West, or Kansas border. Here Cole and fifteen men met sixty of the Kansas Jayhawkers, in the sumac, at the head of the lanes, when Younger cried out, "Boys, charge them upon every hand," when the two commands came together with unsheathed

(*82*)

sabres, drawn revolvers and whistling bullets. The contest lasted for about half an hour, and was hotly contested. It was a dashing fight upon horseback, in which many a saddle was emptied on the part of the Jayhawkers, as well as upon the Rebel side.

There were men with the Jayhawkers whom Cole and his men recognized as those whom they had long wanted to meet in deadly conflict, and now an opportunity offered itself. Although the force of the enemy was four times as large as Younger's, he and his men believed they would be able to send to their final resting place many of the Jayhawkers, where they would no longer be murdering and plundering. After the fight raged a few moments the men became scattered, and each and every one looked out for himself. At last Cole caught the eye of one whom he longed to meet, and the sight of him nerved him up to the very highest pitch, and he determined to kill him or die in the attempt. He knew this fellow's hands were dyed in the blood of his murdered father, and he made a dash at him, firing as he went. The fellow wheeled his horse and dashed over the fence, partly knocking it down, and then struck across the field, Younger following him. Cole's horse proved the fleetest, and the Jayhawker was soon overtaken and fell lifeless from his saddle. Younger then returned to the fight in the edge of the brush, and getting up with the boys yelled out: "Boys, I got my main man! Give the damn thieving cutthroats death on every hand!" Younger and his men by this time had got into the edge of the oak timber. Younger, while endeavoring to get another of his main enemies, run his horse over a post-oak brush, with a very large and thick crown, in which he fell, throwing Younger and got away

(*83*)

from him. He then rose up and crept after his man on foot.
The fellow's horse had became entangled in some grape
vines, and the rider was endeavoring to extricate him when
Younger shot him dead. Mounting the Jayhawker's horse,
Cole returned to the fight. A good many of the Jayhawkers had fled from the field. The remainder and Younger's
men were hard at it, though some were killed and others
wounded. At the close of the fight Al. Shepard's horse, one
of Cole's men, was seen to fall. At this moment Younger
looked up the lane and saw Jennison's command approaching, when he ordered his men to follow him. They then
charged a small squad of Jayhawkers in the mouth of the
lane, who broke over the fence and fled through the field,
when he passed on. About half way down the lane, south,
in a sumac grove, in a hollow, they came upon a small
squad of Jennison's men, who seemed to be watering their
horses. The meeting was unexpected on both sides, though
Younger has his eye to business, and at once poured a shower
of bullets into them, when they broke back up the lane,
Younger and his men following and firing upon them.
Upon coming to a lane at the end of the one they were in,
they took east, while Younger and his men turned to the
right. In the fight Younger lost three men killed and five
wounded, the wounded recovering in a short time. The
Federal loss was eleven killed and seventeen wounded. It
was now about nightfall, and Younger returned to Quantrell's camp.

Jennison and his men camped at the farm house where
Younger and his men were eating dinner when the Jayhawkers came upon them. The treatment the family received at the hands of the Jayhawkers was terrible in the

extreme. They pastured down the golden grain, burned the fencing, destroyed the family provisions, burned the dwelling house, and took all the stock of value on the premises. Al. Shepard was supposed to be killed, for the last Cole saw of him, he and his horse were on the ground in the brush. After Younger and his men arrived at Quantrell's camp, and were relating the fearful little fight they had that day with the Kansas Jayhawkers, and had partaken of some refreshments, and were quietly smoking their corncob pipes, regretting the loss of their brave companions, Cole remarked: "Poor Al., how bravely he fought, but after all, poor fellow, he had to be cut down. His loss as a soldier is irreparable." While thus talking over the past, and viewing the future as best they could, one of the camp guards cried out: "Halt there, and give the countersign!" "I havn't got it," replied the approaching man upon horseback in the thicket. Cole Younger heard the voice, knew it, and jumped up from where he was sitting, smoking his pipe, and said: "There is no hell if that ain't Al. Shepard." Sure enough, it was him, mounted on a spirited charger. He reported that at the close of the fight his horse became entangled in the brush and fell, at the same time he was struck by a straggling ball. Seeing his friends had left and night was approaching, he concealed himself in the brush until dark, and then captured another horse from the enemy. As they had killed his, he thought they were entitled to furnish him another. He kept concealed until about eight o'clock, when he could hear the Jayhawkers at the farm house turning their horses out to graze upon the wheat. Some unsaddled their horses, while others were turned loose with the saddles upon them, and the bridles taken off and fastened to the horn of the saddle. The horses were scattered through the field, and discovering one good one, as he thought, some distance from the rest, he succeeded in coaxing him to be quiet until he secured him, and then took the bridle from the saddle and put it on, when he mounted and made his way to camp.

Surrounded in a Deserted Building.

During the summer of 1862, while they were out on a scout, Quantrell and fifteen of his men took shelter in an old vacated house, in Jackson county, Missouri. About forty Kansas Jayhawkers got on their trail some time previous, and overhauled them shortly after entering the house. Quantrell had built a fire and was drying his blankets. Their horses were hitched about the house. Some of the men were yet holding their horses. Several were in the house with Quantrell, and one was dancing a jig, when all at once the cry came from every side of the house, "Surrender, you damn thieves." Quantrell said to his men, boys, the Red Legs have got us completely surrounded. "God damn you, come out and surrender, or we will kill every one of you," was again sounded in their ears, uttered by the leader of the Jayhawkers. Quantrell asked for three minutes time to consult with his men, which was granted. During the three minutes time allowed them, Quantrell's men recapped their guns and pistols, folded up their blankets, etc., and before the time given them had expired they were ready to scatter death and destruction among the Jayhawkers. Quantrell said to his men, "Boys, we must charge through them, and as soon as we get safe in the saddle open fire upon them." Cole Younger said, "Captain,

(86)

if you have no objections, I will lead the charge." "All right," replied Capt. Quantrell. Younger rushed from the house, mounted his horse, and turned the head of his animal towards the head of the Red Leg column, with a dragoon pistol in each hand, followed by the men. He then clapped spurs to his horse and made a dash for the head of the Red Leg column. By this time the pistols of Younger and the men were being emptied in the ranks of the supposed victorious Jayhawkers, who, three minutes before, had been consulting in their own minds how they would put Quantrell and his men to death. But a few moments time upon the battle-field, often changes the fortunes of the day. The striking of the head of their column turned it to the right, when Younger charged right through, followed by his men. Much damage was inflicted upon the ranks of the enemy, while none of Quantrell's men were killed. Younger killed two men himself. Many of the enemy were killed and wounded. Three of Quantrell's men were slightly wounded. The charge was a complete success and Quantrell and his men made good their escape. The fight lasted but a moment, but while it was going on was extremely lively.

Younger Escapes, Losing His Horse, Coat, etc.

In the month of January, 1863, in Jackson county, Missouri, Cole Younger stopped at the house of a friend to stay for the night, the weather being quite cold, and four inches of snow on the ground. He had been in the woods all day, while the snow was falling. At night it ceased snowing and the weather became very cold. After dark he rode close to a cornfield, tied his horse and went into the field to procure some corn for the animal. The field belonged to a friend of the Confederate cause, and he felt no compunctions of conscience in taking a small amount of corn. The old gentleman was yet at home, as he was, at that time, like a great many others, who sympathized with the Southern cause. He had been forced to take the iron-clad oath, or one similar to the one known by that name, and by complying with its provisions the Federals promised him protection. The oath was frequently administered in order to keep them under subjection, yet, nevertheless, the cutthroat militia would come upon them with the plea that they had been feeding bushwhackers and shoot them down like wolves. This is the kind of civil war that was carried on in Missouri, by the militia bands, which were made up, as a rule, of the very worst class of men in the State.

But, to come directly to the point, this friend of Youngers was feeding his cattle upon the side of the field where Younger had fed his horse, and thus it will be perceived that any morning the stock would blot out all traces of any one having been there to feed his horse. After feeding, Younger would go into the stock trail, which led up to the barn, and went into the house to stay over night, as it was very cold, and he concluded the Federals would not be apt to move around much that night. Younger was sitting by the fire and had pulled off his coat and boots, preparatory to going to bed. It was then about nine o'clock. The dogs had kept up a barking for some time, and the gentleman of the house had gone to the door several times, but could not hear anything but the stock tramping around, apparently hunting shelter from the cold wind. It was not snowing, but the clouds were thick and heavy. Not a star was to be seen. While Younger was thus sitting by the fire, all the family having gone to bed, except the gentleman of the house, he and his friend happened to hear the latch of the gate open. Instantly Cole sprang up and made for the back door. He had no time to get his boots or coat. He opened the door and went into the back yard. As he did so the landlord made a terrible ado with a dog, apparently in the back room, where the militia supposed, hearing the noise, the man was trying to get out to enable Younger to go to bed. But really he was only trying to secrete Younger's coat and boots from the gaze of the soldiers when they entered the house. The militia came to the door with cocked guns and pistols in their hands, and when the door was opened they covered the gentleman of the house, saying: "Where is that damned Cole Younger?" "I have not seen him," was the reply, "for months, though I heard my wife say he was here this morning. He stopped here and made my wife get him something to eat, or, rather he got it himself, by going to the safe and helping himself to as much as he wanted," replied the gentleman of the house, "and I was going up in the morning to report the fact, and would have been up this afternoon but I had no feed out of the field for my hogs, and have been shucking corn all day. Under the circumstances I thought it would make no difference." They replied, "Oh, no," and uncovered him with their pistols and guns, "but we must search your house." "All right," replied the gentleman. The leader of the squad remarked: "I guess we won't find anything in the shape of Younger, for you have told us a very straight and reasonable tale." Younger's coat and boots had been thrown in an old box and a lot of carpet rags thrown over them, thus effectually hiding them from view. The house was thoroughly searched, but no traces of Younger were to be found. The leader said, "We thought we had him, sure, as we found his horse tied to the back of your field to-night, and got him." "I do wonder!" replied the host. "Yes we did," replied the leader of the squad: "he was seen by one of our friends, near dark, in the woods, half a mile north of your field, and this fact was reported. When seen by the good Union man, he and his horse were under a clump of brush, Cole Younger having his back towards him." "Might it not have been some one else?" asked the gentleman. "Oh, no," replied the leader, "this man knows Cole Younger too well to be mistaken. At the time he saw him he seemed to be very cold, and was stamping his feet upon the ground. We went to the place and struck his horse's track and followed it to where he tied and fed, and supposed he had come to your house or barn to sleep." "Well, he may be in the barn now," replied the gentleman. "No, he is not," replied the leader, "we have been all over the hay and oats in the barn loft, he is not there." "Oh, well," replied the farmer, "he may be in a shock of fodder in the field." "Well," replied the leader, "if he is he will have to stay there to-night, but we will give him a round in the morning. It is too cold to-night to hunt any further." The farmer remarked that "he seemed to be nearly starved that morning, as his wife told him that he ate very greedily." "We will give him bullets to eat in the morning," replied the leader, and off they went.

Cole Younger, after passing out the back door, went on

through the garden, and got on top of a plank fence, on which he walked the whole length, about half a mile, to a county road, on which there was always considerable travel, it being a neighborhood road. Younger jumped from the fence and landed in the middle of the road, which, to his great delight, was pretty well tramped up by people and stock passing after the snow had ceased falling. He knew of a friend on this road, two miles off, and walked there as rapidly as possible. He reached the house about twelve o'clock that night and knocked at the door, when he was answered, "Who is there?" Cole replied, "A friend." The man at once recognized Younger's voice and got up and opened the door. Younger then told his friend what had happened to him. His friend replied, "I see you are badly off for a coat and a pair of boots, and must be near frozen." "Oh, no," replied Younger, "I can stand a great deal; I am used to roughing it." "Where is your horse," inquired his friend. "I tied him at the back of Mr.——'s field and fed him after night, and I guess they have got him; at least I shall not go back to look for him. I want you to furnish me a coat, boots and horse." "I can furnish you a coat and let you have my Sunday boots," replied his friend, "but the horse I cannot, as the Federals will find it out." "Oh," said Younger, "that can easily be arranged so as to screen you from harm. Just go to them in the morning and report that your horse was stolen last night, with saddle and bridle, and they will quickly accuse me of it." "That will do," said the friend, and straightway he went to the stable, put the saddle and bridle on the horse, then returned to the house, telling Younger that the horse was in the stable, all ready. Cole then put on the coat and boots

(*91*)

and was soon off, and by sunrise was in Lafayette county, twenty-five miles distant.

Successfully Trapped.

In July, 1873, while Cole Younger and eighteen men were in a creek bottom, in Jackson county, Missouri, Younger discovered on the prairie, about one mile distant, a company of the Missouri Militia making for a farm house, as was supposed. Younger and his men kept their eyes upon them until they arrived at the house and began to dismount. They were about thirty in number. Cole eagerly watched them, to ascertain, if possible, their movements. At length he said, "Boys, by properly managing it, I believe we can get a few of them." "Well," replied one of the men, "how shall we go about doing it?" "My plan is this," said Younger, "We will drop down in the heavy timber, in the creek bottom, along the road, and arrange ourselves in the following manner: Divide the men into two squads upon each side of the road, opposite one another. One squad to drop back in the brush ten or fifteen paces; the other half to pass on down the road sixty or one hundred yards in advance of the first party, secreted and situated similarly. Then send two men up the main road which leads by the house, and as those two men near the house the militia will discover them and put in full charge after them, and when those two men see them coming to fire on them and wheel and take back down the road, and they will, I believe, at once come to the conclusion that they are deserters, aiming to make their way home, and will exert themselves to the utmost to overtake and arrest them; the two men sent out to retreat back to where we are stationed, passing on through, and when those stationed furthest up the road find that they have all passed by, to fire on them from a kneeling position, thus allowing the bullets from each side to pass over our heads and horses; and as soon as the rear men commence firing, those in front to follow in like manner." Every man present signified his acceptance of the proposed plan, and at once two volunteers rode out, signifying their willingness to act as decoys to draw the militia into the trap, planned by Cole Younger's cultivated soldierly thought.

Up the road went the two decoys, mounted upon two very beautiful and fleet chargers, who were so full of spirit that they kept champing on their bits, and in a few moments two shots were heard up the road, not far from the farmhouse where the militia were seen to stop. In a few moments the secreted and awaiting Rebels heard and saw their two cavalrymen coming down the road, with revolvers in hand and firing in the rear of them. On they came and passed through the trap, followed by the militia, and as soon as the last one had passed in, the rear men opened fire on them, which was immediately followed by those in front. Nine dead and wounded men lay in the road in a few moments. Four chanced to escape out of the trap. One of those who were killed was well known to Younger. He was a good man, but had been persuaded to join the militia. Younger regretted his death, but it was now too late. When Younger looked upon his lifeless body he almost shed tears. He was a warm personal friend of Cole Younger. Several of the horses belonging to the militia were killed and wounded. Not a single one of Younger's men was either killed or wounded.

The Independence Fight.

On the first of August, 1862, Quantrell sent a dispatch to Cole Younger to meet him eight miles east of Independence. At this time Younger was camped near the farm of Mr. Thomas Talley, on Cedar Creek, in Jackson county, having about forty men under his command. After reading the dispatch he ordered his men to mount their horses. It was then about five o'clock in the evening. He at once proceeded to carry out orders, and rode off at a rapid rate, making a circuit of about twenty miles in order to get around the Federal post, and reached his destination in an almost incredible short space of time. They were then eight miles east of Independence, which they designed attacking at daylight. The federal force at Independence numbered about six hundred men, under the command of Col. Buel. Quantrell took the main road for Independence, placing Cole Younger in the advance. When near the town a halt was made for a short time, after which, according to previous arrangements, Cole Younger led the charge. He charged through the town, directly under the fire of the guard, who were stationed at the bank. At the first round Kit Childs, one of his men, was killed, Col. Hughes, a Confederate Colonel, who chanced to be with them, was also killed shortly afterwards.

Younger led his advancing party on through the town to the main Federal camp, stationed about one mile west of Independence, where he made a bold and daring charge upon them, driving them, some five hundred strong, into the woods and behind a stone fence, near by. Younger then dismounted his men; a general engagement was com-

(94)

menced; advantage was taken of trees, stumps, &c., and a lively fire was kept up on the enemy. In the meantime, Quantrell was engaging those in the vicinity of the bank. Younger kept up a lively fire until about 11 o'clock, when he made a charge upon them and gained possession of the stone fence, which enabled him to keep up a continuous fire upon their then exposed ranks, which continued but a short time until the Federals made an unconditional surrender. He then ordered them to stack their arms, and, after placing a small guard over them, took his main force and rejoined Quantrell at the court-house, which was opposite the bank.

Younger then took his men and arranged them in the rear of the bank, so as to effectually prevent the Federals from firing upon them, while he and another man procured a lot of hay or straw from a barn near by and proceeded to fire the bank at a door in the rear of the building. After the bank was discovered to be on fire the Federals attempted to put it out, but a few well directed shots caused them to hastily retreat. At length the building got well under way of the flames, when Col. Buel and his men, about one hundred, surrendered unconditionally. During this whole engagement the loss of Quantrell's men footed up but nine, while those of the Federals amounted to 83. All the prisoners were then brought together and placed in line, after which they were paroled. After this Quantrell and his men proceeded to the stables where the Federal horses were, intending to select the best, and while looking at and examining them, an Irishman, a paroled prisoner, who was sitting on the fence, said to Cole Younger, "Be jabers, and I believe you're the same man that hollored so much." Younger replied, I yelled out several times. "Faith and I likes your looks better than any of them other fellows, and if you will come with me I will give you Spile Driver, the best horse on top of ground; he will carry you any place." Younger at once agreed to go and see the horse, and found him to be an excellent one, and at once appropriated him to his own use. He kept him the remainder of the war, although he was not kep in active service all the time. Quantrell withdrew his men from town and went into camp at old Mr. Walker's, some eight miles southwest of Independence, from which place he sent Cole Younger to meet Gen. Cockrell, who had dispatched Quantrell that he was coming in from the South, to recruit.

The Battle of Lone Jack.

On the 15th day of August, 1862, the day after the Independence fight, Cole Younger, with about forty men, started to meet Cockrell, going as far as the Sny Hills, the first day, where he stopped for the night. The next morning he heard firing in the direction of Lone Jack, about nine miles distant, and at once went to the scene of battle, getting there at the time the battle raged the hottest, about two hours after it commenced. After arriving at the scene of deadly conflict, and taking a survey of the field to ascertain the position of the Confederate forces, he proceeded to report to Gen. Cockrell, who informed him that he needed cavalry, as all his horses were jadded. Cole Younger then told Cockrell that he had forty men, all well mounted and armed, and then proceeded to carry out the instructions of Cockrell. He took position on the left, in the brush, and did much effective service. Finally, he discovered a company of men off some distance, in the rear, who seemed not to be engaged in the fight. Thinking this strange, as he knew Cockrell had no men that ought to be idle, he rode over to them and asked why they were not engaged in the fight. Their reply was, they had no ammunition. He then told them to hold on and he would get them some, and at once rode back to where his men were in line and gathered up considerable ammunition, his men always carrying an extra supply, and returned back to the company in the rear and distributed it among them. As he was about to leave he met the Captain, and at once discovered, as he thought, that he had been mistaken in the men, and that they were Federal militia, instead of Confederates. Quick as thought he determined to correct the mistake he had made, and told the Captain he had orders from the headquarters to tell him to hold his men in that position until further orders. After some few words with the militia Captain, Cole Younger rode back to his command and made several successful charges before the fight terminated.

Particulars of the Battle.

Much has been said and written about the events which occurred during the late war, but as yet nothing of a definite character has been written about the battle of Lone Jack, Missouri. An eye-witness and participant in the whole affair, furnishes us the following:

The battle was fought on Saturday, the 16th day of August, 1862. Lone Jack is a small village situated in the eastern part of Jackson county, Missouri. About the

first of August, 1862, Col. Bard. Cockrell was commanding a small battalion of Confederate troops then stationed
at the mouth of Frog Bayou, a small tributary of the Arkansas river, which empties its waters into said stream
about fifteen miles below Fort Smith. Fort Smith, as many
are aware, is one of the principal commercial towns of
the State of Arkansas, and is situated upon the right bank
of the Arkansas river, 405 miles from its mouth. From this
place Col. Cockrell advanced with his command, by the
way of Cane Hill, Arkansas, a small inland town, situated
in the western part of the State, upon the Cherokee line. We
camped at this place one day and night, cooking up rations
for our mess. They marched from this place by way of
Cross Hollows, Arkansas, and entered Missouri south of
Newtonia. This is a small village, located in the eastern
part of Newton county, Missouri. At this place the Federals had a Military post established, which was held by
the Missouri Militia. They had the Government stores deposited there for all of their troops then acting in that
part of Southwest Missouri. On the evening of the 12th of
August, 1862, a feint attack was made upon this place,
in order to draw, or cause the enemy to evacuate the small
garrisoned towns along the line between Kansas and Missouri, for this was their stronghold, and all their essentials
and necessaries were here deposited. It was absolutely
necessary that they should hold this place at all hazards,
as if lost it would be the death-knell to those other towns
held in this part of the State, for some months to come.
Their forces stationed at other places in the vicinity, when
Newtonia was threatened, were by orders of the commanding officer of this district, to evacuate and flock to the de-

(98)

fence of Newtonia. For an inland post it was well fortified, being enclosed by a stone fence or a wall five feet
high, and of the proper thickness to shelter them from ordi-
nary assaults from the outside. Inside of this wall was a
stone barn, also surrounded by a stone wall.

After skirmishing with the Federals until nightfall, the
cavalry fell back two miles, feeding the animals and resting until 8 o'clock at night. They then made another feint
on the place, and found out the troops from other towns
were hastening to the defense of Newtonia. Col. Cockrell,
perceiving that his purpose for attacking the place was
fully accomplished, drew off his troops and made a
forced march for Northwest Missouri, passing through the
western tier of counties bordering upon Kansas. Col. J. T.
Coffee had entered Missouri southwest of Springfield, some
days before Cockrell had come into the State, and had proceeded upon that line as far north as Humansville. The
Federal Militia being too numerous, and it becoming rather
uncomfortably hot for his handful of men, from this place
Col. Coffee marched west as far as the west part of St.
Clair county. While here he learned from a small scouting
party of Cockrell's that he, Cockrell, was passing up the
line between Missouri and Kansas, with a batallion of five
hundred men, making his way to Northwest Missouri. Col.
Coffee immediately dispatched a courier to overtake Col.
Cockrell and say to him that he, Coffee, was on a forced
march to overtake him, Cockrell, and wished to act with
him while in the State of Missouri. To this request Col.
Cockrell acquiesced, stopping at Pleasant Gap, Missouri,
until Col. Coffee came up, which was but a few hours afterwards.

Col. Coffee had a command of about two hundred men; Col. Tracey had about two hundred, and Col. Hunter, who had been acting with Cockrell since he entered the State had a small force of new recuits. When the whole force were consolidated they had about nine hundred men.

From this place they made a forced march, aiming to get to Jackson county before the news could be dispatched ahead of the command by the enemy. I would here remark that they did not enter the State for the purpose of fighting battles, unless the safety of the command demanded it. Their sole object was for the purpose of recruiting for the Confederate army of the Trans-Mississippi Department. They had learned while in Arkansas that there were many men in the brush in Missouri who had been driven from their homes and dear ones by the Militia, who had entire control of the State at that time. It was also said that the Militia had threatened every man who was southern in his sympathies and feelings, or sympathized with the cause of the South, with instant death, if they did not come into the posts and surrender themselves to the Federal authorities. Such an order, it was said, had been issued, and this inspired every true patriot who was devoted to the land of his birth, and the cause of his people, and made all feel called upon to rally to the support of their friends and release them from the cruel hands of their oppressors.

By this time recruits in squads of from five to fifteen began to join our command. The Confederate Cavalry entered Lone Jack on the evening of the 15th of August, about six o'clock, halting but a few moments to get what news could be gathered, not even dismounting, and also to ascertain a suitable place to camp that night, as they wished rations for the men and provender for the horses. After the desired information had been obtained, Col. Cockrell led his command on about two miles, to a wooded pasture, northwest of Lone Jack.

This town took its name from a great black jack tree, which stands upon the high prairie a short distance south of town. The tree can be seen to this day, but we learn it has ceased to put forth its foliage, as of yore.

Col. Coffee went into camp about half a mile southwest of Lone Jack, upon the Pleasant Hill road. Col. Tracey camped not far from Col. Cockrell.

About eight o'clock the same evening 985 Federal cavalry entered town, with two pieces of artillery, commanded by Maj. Foster, acting as Colonel. Col. Cockrell had been well acquainted with Maj. Foster before the war, and even up to the time of the breaking out of the war, he having lived in Warrensburg, Mo., the home of Col. Cockrell. He was known to be a brave and resolute man. The Federal troops were mounted on excellent horses, armed with Spencer rifles, Colts' dragoon revolvers, and had two pieces of artillery, being brass pieces, and were a portion of an Indian brass battery of eleven guns. To use their own words, they had been sent out from Lexington, Mo., to capture Quantrell, who had captured Independence, Mo., a few days previous, killing several of the Federal troops. It seemed that word had been sent to Lexington that Quantrell was to be in Lone Jack on the 16th of August, and the Federal authorities believed the information they had received to be authentic, and were still of this opinion until the battle was over. These facts were learned from one of their men who was captured, who was one of their gunners,

(*101*)

and the only one who survived, the balance falling in action. Quantrell was not in the town on the 16th, having gone above Independence with the most of his men about nine o'clock the night previous. Col. Cockrell had received word that Lone Jack was in the possession of the Federals. At this time but few families were living in the town, but those who were there were as true as steel to the Confederate cause. Those ladies, as there was nobody but women and children, were true patriots, and when the Federals endeavored to find out from them where Quantrell and his men had gone to, they knew nothing about it. Not supposing or knowing of any other Confederate troops being in the country, they did not inquire about any but Quantrell's men. As soon as Col. Cockrell had received the information that the Federals were in town, he ordered his men to mount their horses. They then marched out, coming into the road that leads from Lone Jack to Independence. After arriving at a point of timber, at the edge of the prairie, they halted, dismounted, and hitched their horses. The men were then ordered to fall into line, which was done at short notice, and marched directly down the road some distance, and were then formed in line of battle. The line run parallel with the road, on a piece of low land. This was about ten o'clock at night. After remaining in line a short time, the men were ordered to lie down in line upon their arms and await further orders. Col. Jackman gave orders to his men to be silent, as the enemy were expected upon that road.

Jackman said to his men: "Soldiers, there are about one thousand Federal cavalry in Lone Jack, having with them two pieces of artillery. This fact I learned from a citizen of the town, who left there after the enemy came in. They are all well armed and mounted upon good horses. If they don't spy out our whereabouts to-night, we will attack them at early dawn on the coming of the morrow. Men, I feel that we are going to have a hard fight of it, as the enemy is commanded by a very resolute officer, one who knows no fear upon the field of battle, and I suppose his men are picked cavalry-men, selected from different regiments. What leads me to think so is this—they have come out from Lexington in search of Quantrell and his band of braves, and they know full well it will take men of extraordinary nerve to cope with Capt. Quantrell anywhere in Jackson county, and especially in the Sny hills." Some one said, "Colonel, can't we get out of it without a fight?" "No," said the Colonel, "those Federals are now close, in striking distance, and mounted on much better animals than we have; and moreover, they are fat and in excellent plight. The most of ours are jaded down. Therefore, if we were to endeavor to flee from the country, we would be overtaken and the most of us cut down by the enemy. Thus you will see that we are compelled to offer battle in the morning, and we, my brave soldiers, must gain a decided victory over the enemy or leave our bodies upon the field of battle. And I know full well you possess the nerve. Never has nerve yet forsaken you while upon the field of battle, in the face of the invaders of our most happy and prosperous country, where our loved ones dwelt in peace, plenty and happiness. Therefore, if we engage the enemy in battle in the morning, let each and every one of us resolve to conquer or die upon the field, and we will gain a decided victory over the foe, who has caused so many mothers,

(*103*)

wives and sisters to weep and wail over the loss of their dear ones, who have been shot down in cold blood by the thieving, cut-throat militia of Missouri, aided by the Kansas Red Legs and Jayhawkers. The most brutal murders ever recorded in the pages of history are no comparison to some of those committed in Missouri."

This short speech of the Colonel caused an unquenchable flame of patriotism and revenge to burn within the breast of almost every man, many of whom had their dear fathers and affectionate brothers shot down in cold blood, at the dark hours of midnight, as well as by day.

They lay in this position until day began to break in the eastern horizon. Col. Jackman then ordered the men into line. They mounted their horses and marched down the road until they were within a half mile of town; then filing to the left, to the timber or wooded ridge, they dismounted, leaving the unarmed men to take care of the horses, and detailing a squad of 65 men, armed, to guard them. The remainder of the force was ordered into line and led by Col. Jackman down the Lone Jack road, to within 300 yards of the town, to a steam mill. By this time daylight was fast making its appearance. Col. Cockrell was to command the entire field, while Jackman, Tracey and Hunter were to lead the men into action. Tracey was to attack the enemy on the East, and Jackman upon the West, Col. Hunter acting with Jackman. Col. Coffee had not yet come up with his command. Cockrell advanced to within a few yards of the enemy to ascertain their position, and soon returned with the information that the enemy was still asleep and occupied the town, with but one set of pickets out, on the Lexington road, about a quarter of a mile from town. It was determined to attack the enemy at the earliest moment.

Col. Cockrell directed Col. Tracey to cross the Lexington road north of the Federal pickets, and at a certain given signal to attack them with vigor on the east of town. This signal was the firing upon the pickets on the Lexington road. The town stretches away to the south and north with one main street, 60 or 100 feet in width. The business houses and dwellings were strung along on both sides of the street, some two or three hundred yards. Upon the east and west of the town were cornfields, which lay just in the rear of the buildings, with the exception of here and there an idle field, then in grass several feet high. The steam mill was situated in a ravine or hollow, and near by was a beautiful fresh water spring. The ravine took its rise directly south of the mill, some three hundred yards, in the field west of town. Jackman ordered his men to open the fence in the ravine, and then marched his command of five hundred men directly up this ravine until he came in front of the town. Here he halted and formed in line of battle. They were now about 250 yards west of town. The lowness of the ground upon which the line was formed, and the tall, rank weeds upon the rising ground in front, entirely hid the command from the enemy, even if they had been up in camp, but the stillness of their camp plainly told they were yet asleep, and perhaps dreaming of home and the dear ones left behind, all of which they were doomed never more to see on earth. They were now in battle array, ready for the conflict which was about to ensue. Jackman's men were in the height of enjoyment, and jokes were freely passed up and down the line. They soon learned that all was right, and they were already and eager for the word or orders to be given to move upon the enemy.

Jackman walked up and down the line, telling the men as soon as the firing commenced on the Lexington road, north of town, he wanted the entire line to move forward, no man to break ranks, and to move forward in silence, without a cheer from any one. Tracey was moving around upon the east, and the detail, which had been sent to fire on the pickets, had not yet been carried out. It was thought that the attention of the Federals would be drawn in that direction, expecting an attack from that quarter, while Jackman would attack them on the left and rear, and Tracey attack them upon the right. An attack thus made, with vigor and resolution, was expected to crown the Confederate arms with victory in a short time. But there was too much delay in attacking the enemy's outpost.

The sun was now rising from beneath a cloudless eastern horizon, and pouring its golden streams over the flowery prairie, which was so thickly strewn with beautiful blossoms upon every hand, and lighting up the entire landscape with the silvery orb of day. Yet all was apparently still at the distant town, where the foe was slumbering. Yet soon, very soon, blood was to flow, and some of Missouri's bravest sons were to water the earth with their blood.

At length the enemy's camp guard discovered Tracey's troops upon the east. Immediately thereafter the Sergeant of the Guard was called. They could hear the call distinctly. Very soon the camp was aroused from slumber, with the news that Quantrell's men were upon them! This started every man to his feet. They commenced to move out their "bull-dog" guns in order to fire upon Tracey's men, when the detail which had been sent to fire on the pickets at length opened fire. But they had delayed too long. The enemy were fully apprised of their presence. Jackman at once ordered his men forward, telling them to keep silent until they reached the fence in the rear of town. But when the line got within about 70 yards of the fence, the men were so eager for the fight that they raised a yell. This developed their line, and the enemy poured a galling fire into their ranks. They had intended to surprise the enemy, but as matters now stood, their only reliance was on stubborn fighting. Their artillery had opened fire on Tracey's command, and were throwing shells at him in rapid succession; but they were too close to do much execution.

Col. Tracey was struck upon the foot with a piece of shell, and was so disabled that he had to quit the field. But his captains only fought the harder. Tracey's men pressed forward and gained the fence upon the east of town, which was made of boards, and then they had to pass through a perfect sheet of fire to gain the hedge, behind which the Federal troops were; but there was no such word as fail, and on those brave troops rushed until they had driven the enemy from their position. They then took refuge in the buildings of the town. As the Rebels took possession of the west of the town they found the enemy directly in front, with their line of battle formed in the rear of their horses, which were hitched to the town fencing and served to shelter them from the musketry. But as soon as fire was opened Jackman discovered that they were massing in the rear of the horses, and he ordered his men to shoot them down. One round cleared away the animal breastwork.

Assassination and Robbery of Col. Henry W. Younger

Most of the horses were shot dead, and those that were wounded broke loose and dashed wildly through the enemy's lines, who fled to the farm houses. Some took shelter in the out-houses, while others formed behind them.

This sheltered them from Jackman's fire upon the west, but exposed them to Tracey's upon the east. Jackman's and Tracey's lines were about one hundred yards apart, and the enemy between. So the reader can see that the Confederate lines were so close together that the fire from one could not help but take effect upon the other. As the enemy would show themselves at the doors and windows of the house, the Rebels kept up a lively fire. Now and then could be seen squads of them rushing from behind the buildings, as Jackman's men would pour volley after volley into them, or Tracey's men, as the case might be. Their artillery was still playing upon the Confederates, consequently orders were given and gallantly obeyed, to a part of Jackman's and Tracey's men, for those gallent sons of Missouri to charge the guns. As they rushed boldly forward, they poured volley after volley into the gunners, at only a few feet distant. It looked like a hand-to-hand fight. Those cannoneers were brave men indeed; they stood to their guns until the last moment—all cut down but one.

The artillery was at length captured. The battery was planted alongside of a long wooden blacksmith-shop, where they concluded to make a stand and defend their hard gained prize; but the enemy could not think of giving up those beautiful guns without an effort upon their part to recapture them, consequently they formed a company or two in rear of the shop, a portion of their men taking possession of the shop and poured a deadly fire into the

Confederates, at a few paces, which was hotly contested for a few moments. Finally, finding resistance no longer prudent, the Confederates fell back to their former position, and kept up a brisk fire upon the enemy. Jackman's men had gone into battle with only six rounds of ammunition. It had now given out. He had sent a detail after ammunition, but it had not yet arrived. Finally, Jackman ordered his men to quit the field and retire to the ordnance wagon, where they could draw ammunition. On arriving at the ordnance wagon, we found that the ammunition had been served. The detail was sitting upon a wagon mule, with the box which contained the cartridges before him upon the animal. Some of the command, however, never left the field. They had got into the cartridge boxes of the dead enemy, and were sending back to them their ammunition in hot haste. It was not long, however, until the Confederates were supplied with ammunition, when they returned to the battlefield and took possession of their old position and opened fire upon their combatants at close quarters. The hour looked critical for the Confederates. But all seemed to believe that victory would yet perch upon their banner. At times it seemed that the victory had been won.

The enemy seemed much better prepared now than at first. They had secreted themselves in every possible place in the town, and were sitting with cocked guns in hand waiting for an opportunity to discharge them at close range. They were upon the west side of the town, in a hotel, a large two story building. This building was completely crowded with them, and as Jackman's men came upon the field, many of them were cut down by the enemy's fire from the hotel building. Col. Jackman, Capt. Bryant, Capt. Bradley and three or four soldiers, had come upon the field and were standing close together, about forty paces from the hotel building, when a volley came from the windows of the second-story and cut all down but the Colonel and one other, five men being shot dead, and one slightly wounded. Col. Jackman stepped over the dead and wounded, and looking toward the hotel, his very eyes flashing with revenge, and his cheeks lit up with the red glow which was common with him upon the battle-field. He seemed determined to revenge the blood of the slain— those gallant Captains that had fallen, and in calm but determined words, called out to his men to set the building on fire. A dozen or more raised the yell and made for the building, but several fell in the attempt to fire the hotel. The building, however, was soon on fire, and very soon wrapped in the flames of the devouring element. Many of their men rushed out with cocked guns in their hands, but the Confederates were also ready and shot them down as they rushed out. Many never left the house, but were burned to death. As the lady of the house attempted to leave the building, having been forced to remain inside by the soldiers, as was afterwards learned, she was shot down in the street. The loss of this Southern lady mortified the Confederates, but they were not aware that she was in the building, and the fatal shot was purely accidental. Their very hearts bled at the sight of her dead body, as many of them had been furnished by her with shelter and provisions. According to the best information obtainable, nine wounded men in the building burned to death.

The battle then raged with all the horrors of war from

(*111*)

one end of the town to the other. It was plainly to be seen
that the forces of the enemy were thinning out much more
so than the Confederates, although they had lost a great
many brave soldiers, though their force was a still formidable one. They were to be seen on the tops of houses,
behind chimneys, and took every advantage of shelter from
the bullets of the Confederates. Yet the Confederates would
pick their men off, and they could be seen dropping from
the tops of buildings with a dull and heavy sound. At
length they commenced running around in every direction,
endeavoring to make their escape, while the Confederates
poured volley after volley into them, and they were cut
down as the grass before the mower. The Confederates
seemed resolved to make it a lasting and decisive victory.
The screams and yells of the men as they came together,
in deadly conflict, made the very earth tremble. Many times
they were not ten paces apart. The battle raged in this
terrible manner for three long hours. Finally, the Federals
were completely hemmed in upon three sides. The only
outlet was upon the south side of town. At length orders
were given to press them at every point, and the Confederates rushed upon them with terrible fury, and for a short
time there was a hand-to-hand fight, almost throughout the
whole field of battle. The screams of the wounded and
dying fell upon every ear. Tongue nor pen could not
portray the scenes of blood. The smoke and blaze of powder brought to mind all the dreadful realities of a very
hell. Brave men on both sides had met in battle, and there
was no disposition to give way so long as the least hope of
victory remained.

The Federals at length became satisfied there was no

(*112*)

longer any use to contend for victory, their comrades having stood up bravely in the fight, but were being cut down like grass before the scythe. At length they commenced to retreat through the only avenue left them for escape, which was south of town. Here they made a short stand, solely with the view of getting some of their dead and wounded off the field, and were soon seen flying, panic-stricken, making their way, headlong, for Lexington, on the Missouri river, with nearly one-half of their original number lost, the remainder terribly demoralized. Thus was Col. Foster honorably defeated.

The principal part of the troops engaged in this terrible battle, on the Confederate side, were from the counties of Bates, Vernon and St. Clair. St. Clair county lost in killed and wounded, 37 men. The entire Confederate loss was 36 killed dead on the field of battle, and 134 wounded, many of which were mortal. Two months afterwards the Confederate loss amounted to 72, including those who were killed dead on the field, and those who died from the wounds received in the battle. The Federal loss, as reported, was 136 killed on the field of battle and 550 wounded, many of whom died afterwards. Many of the Federal wounded were carried off the field during the fight, and sent to Lexington. Col. Foster himself was wounded in several places, and his brother, Capt. Foster, then acting Major, was mortally wounded, and died shortly after.

In a conversation with one of Col. Foster's men, whom we met at Monegaw Springs, in the autumn of 1869, he said one regiment, the one he was in, lost 450 men in all, killed and wounded. His regiment was never reorganized

(*113*)

afterwards. He said he was in Company C, and their company came out of the fight with only two sound men.

The Confederates carried those fine brass guns to Arkansas. All told, the battle lasted about six hours. After the battle the Confederates fell back two miles southwest, to cook rations, procure forage, and care for the wounded. It was then about noon. They then took up their line of march for the South, hotly pressed by the Federals, who had, in the meantime, received new recruits. Some of the Confederates had lost so much sleep that they fell from their horses on the route and were picked up by the enemy, who, when they learned the condition of the men, did not attempt to secure them as prisoners, and the result was that as soon as many of them had secured sufficient rest and sleep to restore them to their proper minds, they rode off and made their way to their old comrades in Arkansas. The Federals followed them until the Arkansas line was reached.

Col. John T. Coffee was accused of acting cowardly at the battle of Lone Jack. This is an error. It is true Col. Coffee was not in the battle, but it was unavoidable on his part, as he was misled on the night of the 15th of August from his camp on the Pleasant Hill road, south of town. His aim was to reach Cockrell's command that night. Nearly all of that country, at that time, was fenced up, upon the main road. There were large gates through which travellers had to pass. Coffee and all of his men were unacquainted in that part of the country, consequently they became bewildered in the darkness of the night and could not find the desired route. The Colonel finally succeeded in obtaining a guide, who proved to be an enemy.

After the fellow had led Col. Coffee miles and miles in the contrary direction, about two o'clock in the morning he deserted him, leaving him in a 200 acre cornfield. Here he was compelled to stay until morning. When day broke the Colonel was informed by a lady that his guide had led him southwest of Lone Jack, instead of northwest, where he wanted to go, to join Cockrell's command. Coffee was now ten miles from Lone Jack. He, however, started in that direction, hoping to hear something of Col. Cockrell. After marching within six miles of Lone Jack, and hearing nothing of Cockrell, he stopped to rest his men. Hearing no report of fire arms, he finally concluded that Cockrell had left that part of the country. But while breakfasting his men, two men, who seemed to be dispatch bearers, came up. On questioning them, Col. Coffee found out they belonged to Quantrell's command, and had been sent out upon a scout. Coffee asked them if there were any troops in the direction of Lone Jack. Yes, was the reply, Col. Cockrell has been fighting the Federals ever since sun up this morning. Haven't you heard the artillery? The Colonel replied, I have not. Coffee then ordered his men to mount their horses. This was about ten o'clock. Coffee went within about a half mile of the battle-field, dismounted his men, and hastened to the scene of the conflict. When he arrived the enemy were flying in every direction, the battle was over, and the brave enemy was defeated.

After the battle of Lone Jack, Cole Younger and his men disbanded, temporarily, well knowing that the whole Federal force within striking distance would completely scour the country.

Assassination of His Father.

About the first of September he heard of the murder of his father, and at once determined to go and look once more upon his face, though cold in death. Quantrell tried to induce him not to go, telling him that he certainly would be killed, as there was no doubt they were on the watch for him, expecting him to return home. But go he would, let the consequences be what they may, and when Quantrell saw this was Younger's determination, he urged him to take a detail with him. But this Cole thought to be an unwise movement, and felt satisfied he could do much better alone. The death of his father sorely grieved him; he could not rest easy, and a bitter feeling of revenge showed itself upon every feature of his face, and was manifest in every utterance when speaking of him to whom he was greatly attached. He made the trip alone, looked upon the remains of his beloved father, never shedding a tear, and, placing his right hand upon his cold forehead, without uttering a word, resolved within his own mind to revenge his death or lose his own life in the attempt.

After returning to camp he called his men together and related to them the circumstances of the murder and robbery of his dear old father, and all for the sake of a few hundred dollars, endeavoring to arouse all their bitter feelings, and asked them to assist him in his efforts to wreak vengeance upon those guilty of the heinous crime. After this he was continually on the alert with twenty picked men.

The Pleasant Hill Fight.

On the 5th of October, 1862, while roaming around, he chanced to ride to Pleasant Hill, and on entering the town learned that Col. Neugent was there with forty men. After deliberating a moment he concluded to give him battle. The war whoop was at once raised, and he dashed into town and among Neugent's men, scattering them in every direction, killing and wounding many, while he did not lose a single man. The town of Pleasant Hill is situated in Cass county, Missouri.

Another Skirmish.

On the 10th of October, 1862, Jennison and Anthony, two notorious Kansas Jayhawkers, made a raid into Jackson county, Missouri, burning houses, stealing horses and almost everything else of value they could conveniently carry off, and murdering indiscriminately. They marched under the black flag. Quantrell was on the lookout for them, while Younger dogged Jennison at every turn. At length Jennison received large reinforcements and the whole country was filled with Jayhawkers. A general sortie was kept up by Quantrell's men, and small parties of the Jayhawkers were frequently cut off, while their pickets were engaged whenever an opportunity offered. Jennison made a dash on Quantrell one day in an open field, when Quantrell rode over a hill and watched an opportunity to strike with telling effect, and when followed by Jennison, he made a desperate charge on the Federal forces. Cole Younger led the charge, while Quantrell held in reserve a

(*117*)

force of men ready to assist or strike in another direction, as circumstances should develope themselves. Younger, in leading the charge, held a pistol in each hand and guided his horse by holding the reins in his teeth. In making the charge he was several times heard yelling: "give them hell, boys." His brave little band nobly rushed to the front, spreading death and destruction on every side, which caused the Jayhawkers to flee, and fall back on their reserve forces. When the Federals were forced to retreat, Younger rode off to where Quantrell was and they consulted as to the best plan to be pursued. It was finally determined that as the men and horses were tired and hungry, to disband for a few days, in order to gain rest and procure food for both man and beast, as both had but little of either for several days. The men were then divided up into small squads, under faithful leaders.

Horse Stealing.

About this time there seemed to be a well organized band of horse-thieves roaming through the country, and many horses were stolen. Finally, Quantrell determined to put a stop to it, and Cole Younger was detailed to keep watch in Cass county, Missouri, for the purpose of capturing a band of thieves, while Quantrell watched Jackson county, Missouri. On the 20th of October Younger went to Austin, in Cass county, for the purpose of capturing a band of thieves, which was finally accomplished, and he turned them over to Quantrell, who dealt with them as their crimes deserved.

Quantrell Goes South.

Quantrell, as usual about this season of the year, went South, leaving Cole Younger and George Todd, each of whom had a company of men, to act for themselves, but their forces were consolidated and concert of action had whenever it was deemed advisable.

In Prepared Caves.

Cole Younger then took his men and went into camp on Cedar Creek, in caves or dirt houses prepared for that purpose, where he remained for several weeks, and until a severe snow storm visited that section of the country. This had the tendency to very materially interfere with his successfully eluding the pursuit of the Federals, as his whereabouts could be easily found out by tracks through the snow, for provisions and forage were short, and he was compelled to send out for both. When they were at length compelled to visit corncribs, &c., after leaving they would get some member of the families on whose premises they went, to drive the cattle around, drag over their tracks in the snow with felled trees, and resort to every possible strategy to cover up the route they had taken.

A Spy in Camp.

About this time a spy came into camp, who claimed to have belonged to the Confederate army. He told a pitiful and plausible story of the inhuman treatment he had received at the hands of the Federals, by whom he had been taken prisoner. His story of wrongs seemed to impress itself upon Cole Younger, and he believed what the fellow

(119)

told him. George Todd, by some means, had received unfavorable reports about the man and at once went and told Younger what he had heard, at the same time advising him to either shoot him or else turn him out of camp. But Younger's sympathy had become too much enlisted for the stranger, and he not only told Todd that he should remain in camp, but also said that he would protect him. Upon investigation it was found that Jobe McCorkell, one of Younger's men, had served with him in the Confederate army. Younger, taking the statement of McCorkell to be correct, was still further satisfied that the man was not a spy.

On the morning of the 10th of December, 1862, Younger's visitor reported to him that he had received intelligence that his wife was very sick, and asked permission to visit her. At first Younger hesitated to grant his request, but finally consented, telling him he must not be gone over two hours. The stranger departed, but he had scarcely left camp before a general discussion arose among the men as to whether he was true or false, many determining in their own minds that there was something about him they did not fancy, and who put it down as their firm belief that he was a spy, sent there for the purpose of betraying them. Some of them seemed to be so well satisfied in their own minds that the fellow was sent into camp for a purpose, that they offered to bet he would not return. At this time the men were busily engaged in currying and feeding their horses, playing cards, &c. One of the men, named Oliver Shepherd, was currying his horse in front of the cave, and his horse kept up such a smelling and looking about that he called Younger and told him some-

thing was wrong. Younger told him that was all imagination, but he insisted and said, "By God, there is something
up, as my mare keeps smelling, and I think she smells
Feds." Younger then remarked that he supposed it was
Todd coming, as he was looking for him to come up
about that time. Shepherd replied: I know my mare too
well for that, I know she would not make such demonstrations unless there were Federals around. Younger then
glanced over the ridge, and at a short distance discovered a body of men approaching with an officer in front,
who he at first took to be Todd. Younger than called to him,
Is that you, Todd? He received no reply, and at once
ordered his men into line, as infantry, they not having
time to mount their horses. About the time the line was
formed, Noah Webster, one of Younger's men, discovered
a body of men in their rear. Just at this moment the officer
commanding those who were approaching in front, sang
out: All right, Cole, we are Todd's men.

By this time Younger felt satisfied that they were Federals, and at once gave orders to his men, "Let into them,
boys." As the fire was opened upon those in front, the rear
column opened fire on Younger's men, killing three of
them. A desperate fire was kept up on those in front, until
at length the Federals made a bold and daring charge
upon Younger. The latter, seeing he was completely surrounded, and knowing full well that his visitors had en-
trapped him, at once resolved to cut his way out or die in
the attempt. Leading his men on the double-quick down
the hollow, he forced his way through the Federal column
in front, when they closed up in his rear and pursued. He
then made a rapid retreat. He had not retreated far, how-

ever, until he discovered that the sleet upon the snow was so slippery that a rapid retreat could not be made, and the men were forced to pull off their boots and throw them away. While they were doing this, they were under a heavy fire. After a forward movement was again commenced, one of the men called out to Younger that he could not get one boot off. Younger then halted the men and went and pulled off the remaining boot himself. The Federals were pressing them hard, particularly the cavalry. A running fight was kept up the balance of the day, some four hours. About sundown they struck the main road, leading to Harrison-ville, and followed it some distance, until they came to another road leading off to the right, which they took and kept until they arrived at a bridge, which crossed a creek. Here they jumped from the bridge into the creek, and waded down the creek about a mile, until they came to a stone fence, which they mounted and followed for nearly a half mile, hoping thereby to effectually elude the pursuit of the Federals, which they knew would be made the fol-lowing day. Some time after dark they arrived at a house which proved to be occupied by friendly parties, where they were furnished with something to eat. After supper and resting, the men divided up into pairs and scattered in every direction, instructions being given them to get cloth-ing as best they could, and make their way back to Todd's camp as soon as possible.

In a few days all of Younger's men, except the three killed, found their way back to the camp of Todd, though much fatigued, and with bruised and lacerated feet. The citizens throughout the country supplied them with the required clothing, as best they could. During their retreat, after the Federals had ceased following them, they chanced to discover an old blind horse, which they secured and rode around through some sumac for the purpose of destroying their tracks in the snow. At another time a farmer cut down a tree, leaving the limbs on it, hitched a yoke of cattle to it and dragged it over the snow where they had passed. These little incidents are named in order to show the precaution taken to prevent the Federals making a successful pursuit the next morning. At the time they were attacked most of their horses were running around loose, and when the firing commenced the greater portion of them made for their homes, as nearly all lived close to camp. The citizens, learning of the affair, took some pains, as did Todd's men also, to gather them up. In a short time they were all mounted again.

Younger Gets a Better Horse.

On the 20th of January, 1863, Cole Younger and a companion started to go home, near Lee's Summit, when they met three Federals in the road, two white men and one negro. Younger and his partner not being very well mounted, at once conceived the idea that the present offered an excellent opportunity to secure better animals, and when they got within shooting distance of the Federals, opened fire on them, when they broke and ran away. After pursuing them some distance they came to a house, in front of which was standing a fine horse, with a lady's saddle on. Younger halted alongside the fence, dismounted, threw the reins of his horse's bridle over the post, unloosed the horse with the lady's saddle on, mounted, and pursued rapidly until he overtook the negro, when he unhorsed him

(123)

and appropriated his horse and equipments to his own use. He then returned the horse which he borrowed, with a lady's saddle on, and as he did so he was requested to wait a moment, when a Confederate flag was presented him, with the wish that he might carry it to victory on every occasion, which he promised to do. After going home and remaining a day or two, he again returned to camp and reorganized his men.

Arrest of three Miss Youngers.

About the first of November, 1862, the Federal officer in command at Independence, arrested three of the Miss Younger's, sisters of Cole Younger, and placed them in jail, because, as he said, they had fed their brother Cole. Also three or four of Younger's cousins, females, were arrested and kept prisoners at Kansas City, and were in the building which was undermined and fell down, killing eight out of the nine ladies, prisoners at the time. This was one of the most disgraceful and brutal outrages committed during the war. They did not have the courage to openly execute these ladies, but arrested and placed them in the building, which was built of brick, and then secretly undermined it so that it would fall and so mangle them as to cause their death. If we mistake not, but one was killed instantly, all the rest having been bruised and mangled in a horrible manner, and suffering for some time in the greatest agony before death came to their relief. This took place in the winter of 1862-63.

Trap Set to Capture Younger.

Some time in February, 1863, Capt. Davidson, stationed at Harrisonville, sent word to Mrs. Younger to come down and see him, but not being able to go, on account of sickness, she sent him word to that effect and requested him to come out to the farm and see her, which he did. While there he promised her that if she would see Cole and get him to go South, he would give them both a free pass. This she promised to do, as soon as she could send him word. After this Davidson kept a close watch on her house, hoping to capture Cole, thinking he would come home to see his mother. At length word was sent him, Davidson, that Younger was at home, when that same night the

House Was Surrounded by 100 Men,

determined to capture him, dead or alive. Cole rode near the house and then dismounted and hitched his horse in the orchard, after which he cautiously approached the house, in order to ascertain if any soldiers were about. After entering he got Sue, a faithful old negro servant, to stand guard outside, also one of his sisters, but the night being very dark and cold, he determined to risk it without punishing his sister and old Aunty, and, as he said, "would rather fight the Federals than punish them." After all were in the house a short time, a noise was hard outside, but it was concluded that it was the sheep out in the lot. Cole was busily engaged talking to his mother, when a koock was heard at the door. Quick as thought old Aunty threw a bed quilt over her, Cole blew out the light, and slipped up

(*125*)

Shooting of Fifteen Prisoners

behind the old negro, under the quilt. She then went to
the door and opened it, when there stood a squad of
soldiers, with guns cocked and ready to shoot. The old
negro said to them, "Don't shoot; it's me; nothin' but a
poor old nigger." In a moment the guns were dropped, and
after some little conversation she told them that if they
"was gwine to kill the white folks she would git out," and
at once passed out towards the barn. The night was very
dark, and the Federals did not think of or discover the
trick of Younger to make his escape. After getting some
distance from the house, Cole dodged out from his hiding
place and at once made tracks for a more congenial clime.
The old darkey was so much rejoiced at seeing her young
master thus narrowly escape death by and through her
strategy, that she could not help but yell out, "Run, Massa
Cole, for God's sake," which at once attracted the attention of the soldiers in the rear, who fired on him. Had it
not been for this little imprudence of the old negro, the
Federals would not have discovered him making his escape. Quite a number of shots were fired at him, but
without effect, nevertheless they went into the house and
reported him dead, and requested a light, accompanied by
the family, to go and bring him in. Diligent search was
made in the vicinity where he was supposed to be, but his
body could not be found. After remaining but a short
time, apparently, they all went off, but still kept watch at a
respectful distance, thinking he would return to the house,
if not too badly wounded. All this time he was sitting some
distance off, watching their movements, and eager to "get
some of them." Before retiring to bed the old negro procured a bottle of water, mixed with some whiskey, cam-

phor, &c., and then took a light and went out to hunt for her young Massa, Cole, intending, if she should see him, to pass by him and drop the bottle, well knowing that he would need water if he was wounded. She also thought that if she should get close to him he would call her. Although the Federals had departed, apparently, she found that they were still loitering around. The old servant was true and faithful, and would risk her own life to save that of any of the members of the family, but always felt certain that none of the Federals would harm her. Cole did not go near enough to the house to see if they had discovered his horse, as he supposed they would search the premises until they found him. They did not get his horse, however, although dilligent search was made. The next morning the old negro woman took the horse some distance in the direction of the camp, putting it in a safe place where she knew it would be sent to Massa Cole. He arrived safely in camp.

A Lively Brush.

On the 10th of March, 1863, Cole Younger and his men, about 40 in number, went to the blacksmith shop of Mr. Hopkins, near Blue Springs, Jasper county, Missouri, for the purpose of having their horses shod, as spring was about opening, and they were preparing for more active operations. The precautionary step of placing out pickets was taken, and after remaining there some time the pickets returned with the news that the Federals were coming. Younger at once formed his men in the brush, for the purpose of "giving them a round or two," and after the lapse of a few minutes the Federals came in sight, the

commanding officer, Capt. Johnson, some distance in front.
He had about 80 men. The arrangement was that no shots
were to be fired until all were within close range, but one
of Younger's men, when Capt. Johnson rode up within
range, could not resist the temptation of "letting him have
it." Johnson cried out: "Don't shoot, we are Federals,"
thinking those whom he saw were militia. Several shots
were fired at Capt. Johnson without effect. At length, seeing
that his warning words to "friends" were not heeded, he,
doubtless, concluded that he had fallen among enemies,
and at once wheeled his horse and made a hasty retreat to
the rear. Younger, seeing this movement, at once charged
on behind, which caused the Federals to break and run in
every direction. Capt. Johnson fired several shots on his
retreat, which were the only ones fired, not a single other
man of his company discharging a gun. Capt. Johnson
tried to rally his men several times, but all to no purpose.
They were pursued about one mile and a half, through
the timber, and finally rushed into a deep ravine which led
to the creek. Younger's men kept up a lively fire on them
the whole time, and forced them down the ditch until they
reached the back water, when they were compelled to swim
the creek. Near one-half of their number was killed. After
those who escaped uninjured succeeded in getting over the
creek, out of danger, Younger and his men went over the
battle-field to gather up such arms, etc., as they deemed of
service, and take care of those who were still alive.
Finally, a whistle was heard, which clearly indicated that
it was intended as a call, and which was immediately
answered. At length a sanctimonious looking individual
made his appearance and said, "I thought you were all

killed." Younger at once perceived that he had mistaken them for Federals, and drawing his revolver, told him to surrender. He at once wheeled his horse and rode rapidly away. Younger and one of his men fired at him, both shots taking effect, and he fell to the ground a lifeless corpse. An examination of his wounds, proved that one shot broke his neck and the other entered the head. Either was fatal. On searching the body a small Bible and hymnbook were found, when it was at once conjectured that he was a minister. It was afterwards ascertained that he was the identical individual who was travelling around with Johnson, going to houses to eat and sleep, and when he was about to leave would offer up prayers, after which he would ask pay for the same, and if it was not forthcoming immediately, would appropriate such articles he could find to his own use as he desired. This would-be Reverend (?) gentleman had gained considerable notoriety in that section of country for these "little peculiarities," and when it become known that he "had handed in his checks," there was considerable rejoicing. Evidently he had "put on the livery of Heaven to serve the Devil in."

Fight with a Dutch Company.

On the 15th of May, 1863, Cole Younger went down to Lafayette county, Mo., to see his mother, taking with him a few of his men. As they passed down the road they were bushwacked and made a narrow escape, for, if it had been properly managed, not one of them would have escaped death or capture. After this occurrence Younger determined to try this same little game upon those who perpetrated it upon him. It was not long until he ascertained who it was that perpetrated the "joke," and at once laid his plans to "turn the tables on them." While in Lafayette county, Younger was reinforced by Capt. Pool, with about 20 men. When he was ready to leave, Younger sent a man in advance to inform the Dutch officer that he was coming, telling him what road to watch, and to make a certain point by a certain time and by this means completely trap them. The whole plan worked like a charm; the Dutch officer seemed eager to do up the little job, promising that not one should escape this time, etc. Younger was not disappointed in his expectations, and was on hand in time, ready and willing, with outstretched arms, to receive his dear Dutch friends. By the time appointed along came the valiant Dutch company, the chief officer in the lead, with considerable show and bravado. When they had passed just far enough into the trap, Younger let into them, and of all the surprised and terror-stricken men ever seen, they were the worst. They ran in every direction, closely followed by Younger's men, who poured volley after volley into them. About one-half made their escape, the remainder having been killed. The account of the fight, as given by the Dutch who made their escape, was the most terrible ever related. They seemed to have magnified about 40 men into 4,000, and it was impossible to make any of them believe that they were attacked by less than 4,000 men.

Quantrell Returns.

The reader will recollect that we previously mentioned the fact that Quantrell went South, leaving Cole Younger and Todd, each of whom had a company of men, to act for themselves, but in connection with each other, whenever circumstances should require it. Some time during the latter part of May, however, Quantrell returned to his old stamping ground, and at once commenced to reorganize his men and make preparations for active operations.

The Lawrence, Kansas, Raid.

We now come to the famous raid made on Lawrence, Kansas, by Quantrell and his band. This notable and memorable occurrence is yet familiar to thousands throughout the country who were old enough at the time to recollect it. It was heralded all over the country at the time, as the most blood-thirsty, daring and successful raid ever made. The whole thing was admirably planned and well executed, and scarely anything occurred to interrupt the plans of the men who conceived this master stroke of retaliation and revenge, for such it was.

Jim Lane and his band of Kansas Red Legs had burned and sacked the town of Osceola, St. Clair county, Missouri, one of the most thriving and flourishing towns in Southwest Missouri, situated on the Osage river, murdering many citizens, and Quantrell conceived the idea of retaliation for this and other outrages committed by the Jayhawkers, and consequently selected the home of Lane, quite a thriving town in Kansas, as the best suited for that purpose, hoping also to capture and kill him, in retaliation for those murdered at Osceola, and elsewhere, and in this outdone even Lane himself. It was not the South striking against the North, not a deed done in defense of a country's right, or in retaliation for her wrongs, but in revenge for the wrongs committed by one man, armed and

(*132*)

protected in the knowledge of his power, against a mere handful of men, totally incapable of successful resistance. But, desperate character as Quantrell was, he gave orders to his men on entering Lawrence, to "Spare the women and children." He still possessed enough of human feeling to have compassion on youth and beauty. On that bright morning the birds, though disturbed by the noisy tramp of the many horses' hoofs, strange to say, sang just as sweetly as though nothing terrible was going on. The place was wrapped in slumber when Quantrell and his men entered. Defence was useless, and, as if by common consent, the town was left to its fate, and all attempted to escape to the ravine running along the western side. But few reached it, and those few were hunted from one spot to another, half clothed and unarmed.

It was the morning of the 7th of September, 1863, that Quantrell made this memorable dash into Lawrence. But a short time previous he had returned from the South. As soon as he reached his old haunts he commenced to collect his men together and prepare for this raid. His force numbered about 200 men. They were divided into companies, and placed under the command of Cole Younger, Pool, Todd and Quantrell himself, the whole subject to the guidance and control of the latter.

The force was concentrated on Cedar Creek, in Jackson county, Missouri. From Cedar Creek they marched to Grand River, in Cass county, Missouri, and from there they went to Lawrence, Kansas, arriving about daylight. A charge was at once made upon the town, and every Jayhawker they caught, as well as many citizens, were killed. The main body of the troops quartered there were camped

(*133*)

on the opposite side of the Kansas River. Quantrell, on his arrival in town, at once placed a force at the ferry to prevent their crossing, until such time as he was ready to leave. The massacre and destruction of property continued nearly all day. The mournful cry of the widows, the groans of the wounded and dying, the roar of the flames as they lapped from building to building, all united in making up one horrible scene, in which the Guerrilla chief and his men seemed to glory. All of the Guerrillas, save one, left the town unharmed, and he, more unlucky than his companions, was left behind, the victim of his intended victims. His body was left sissing and burning by the side of the very building that he fired, and those who now reside in Lawrence and were there at the time, well remember with feelings of pleasure and revenge, that the remaining citizens hung the body of this one Guerrilla up as a pleasing memento.

The murders, destruction of property, and outrages committed generally, by Quantrell and his men, were bad enough when the truth is told, yet we learn from those who were there at the time, that the facts were largely magnified by the newspaper accounts gotten up immediately thereafter. It has been asserted that women and children were murdered, but such was not the case, save by accident. Men were murdered, without regard to age. The destruction of property on this occasion was considerable. But little was carried off, except clothing and such articles as the men required for use.

Of all the men whom Quantrell most desired to capture and execute, Jim Lane was the man. It is asserted that he succeeded in making his escape into a cornfield, unobserved, where he kept hid until after all danger was over. One story is that he went down into a well, but we are inclined to the opinion that he made his escape into a cornfield, as above given. Some of the friends of Quantrell assert that if Lane had been captured shortly after entering town, the destruction of life and property would have been much less than it was. There may be some truth in this version of the affair, but the public will be inclined to doubt it. It is evident that Quantrell went to Lawrence determined on death and the destruction of property, and he succeeded admirably in his purposes.

Late in the afternoon the Guerrillas of Quantrell who were placed at the ferry to prevent the Federal forces from crossing over to Lawrence, were withdrawn, and all took up their line of march for Missouri. As soon as the raid was made on Lawrence, all the Federal and Kansas State troops within striking distance were notified of the fact and ordered to pursue Quantrell on his retreat, and by the time he was ready to move several thousand troops were on his trail, and nothing but the mere mention of the name of Quantrell, which was always a terror to the Jayhawkers, saved him and his men from total destruction. It was estimated that before he left the State of Kansas, seven thousand Federal soldiers and Kansas militia were in pursuit of him, who were distributed all over the route Quantrell had to travel.

Cole Younger was placed in the rear on the retreat, with his command, and, as may be imagined, he had hot work of it, for the main body of the Federals crossed the river as soon as Quantrell's men left, and, being joined by others, at once commenced pursuit. The worn out condition of both the men and horses belonging to Quantrell's command, rendered them totally unfit for hard service, but the rear reliefs were frequent, as it was almost one continued series of fighting.

John Jarrett, with his command, was the first to relieve Cole Younger, who then took the lead. Dave Pool relieved Jarrett, but he was so hard pressed—by this time large Federal reinforcements had arrived—that he was compelled to give way and his men become badly demoralized. Seeing this, Younger and Todd both went to the rear, and finally succeeded in checking the Federal advance. By this time Quantrell, with the main body of his men, had succeeded in getting far in the advance. The rear forces were then rapidly withdrawn.

At times the retreating forces of Quantrell were almost entirely surrounded—the Federals were like a swarm of bees. Several times he was attacked in the front and rear, and on the right and left. It was indeed a most miraculous escape. At times Quantrell almost gave up the idea of ever being able to get through safely with many of his men. Almost a continuous fight was kept up until they reached Grand River, in Cass county, Missouri, at which point Quantrell ordered his men to scatter in small squads, and this, together with the darkness of the night, caused the Federal forces to halt, when Quantrell made good his escape. In this raid Quantrell lost but few men. No fight or raid of importance again occurred for some time, although many skirmishes followed.

(*136*)

Rev. Dr. Fisher's Experience.

The following is from the Cincinnati Gazette, which was related by the Doctor himself, recently, at a Methodist Preacher's meeting in Cincinnati. The Rev. Dr. was one of Jim Lane's Chaplains during the war. The story, as related by him, is as follows:

"I was always an anti-slavery man of the most 'anti' kind, and after I moved to Kansas, without any prominence having been given to my sentiments by myself, I found myself the object of the most vindicative hatred of the pro-slavery party of the region where I resided. My life was unsuccessfully sought several times. When the war broke out I went as a Chaplain. Most of the male members of my church went to the war, and I went as one of Jim Lane's chaplains.

"The news of my connection with the army, and of my being put in charge of contrabands, who were sent to Kansas, got abroad, and the rebels hated me worse than ever. They got my photograph and distributed it throughout the country, and it was fixed among them that I was to be shot whenever met. Once when I was sent up the river with a body of contrabands, not being well, I went home for a little rest. I was living at Lawrence. The town had a few guns in the armory, and there was an understanding with the farmers of the surrounding country that upon the ringing of an alarm, they should come in and defend the town, but the coming of Quantrell and his men was a complete surprise. When the alarm was rung the arsenal was already captured and on fire. I was in bed, and heard, about 3 o'clock in the morning, horses galloping very rapidly away, and woke my wife, telling her that it was singular that horses should be galloping so fast so early in the morning; but she said she guessed it was some farmers who had been to a railroad meeting the evening before, and were hurrying back to their work. We lay and talked for some time. The children were going out that morning to get some grapes, and my wife thought she would call them earlier than usual, and herein, brethren, I see the hand of Providence. It was not yet daylight, but day was dawning. Having called the children, she went and looked out of the front door, and instantly called me: 'Pa, the Rebels are in town.' I said that could not be; but, nevertheless, I sprang from the bed and ran to the door.

"There they were just across the green, and just then they shot the United Brethren preacher, as he was milking his cow in his barn-yard. I rushed back into the house; my wife caught up her babe; I have four boys; one was on my wife's breast, another was by her side, and the two oldest were twelve and fourteen years old. We all rushed up the lot in which our house stood. Then I left my wife, and with the two oldest boys ran up the hill, but something seemed to tell me that I was running away from safety. So I told the boys to run on, and I would go back to mother. It was then in the gray light of morning, and the Rebels had divided into little squads and were ransacking the town, killing every man they found, and burning houses. My boys separated, the oldest getting with a neighbor's boy, Robert Winton, and while the two were running for life the soldiers saw them and fired a volley, killing poor Bobby and frightening my boy almost to death. He ran in and hid among some graves in the grave-yard. My younger son ran off on the prairie.

"In fixing my cellar I had thrown up a bank of earth near the entrance, and I crept down there and laid myself between the mound of earth and the wall in such a way that the earth would partially screen me. I lay up close to the kitchen floor. I had not been there long, when four of Quantrell's men rode up to the house and demanded admittance. My wife went to the front door and let them in. They demanded whether I was not in the house or in the cellar. She replied: 'My husband and two oldest boys ran off as soon as the firing began.' The leader swore that he knew I was in the cellar. My wife replied that she had two young children by her, and that she did not want any more oaths uttered before them. 'You have doubted my word,' she replied, 'you can look for yourselves.' I lay so near the floor that I could hear every word that was said. The men called for a candle.

"My wife replied that we did not burn candles. Then they

wanted a lantern, but she said we hadn't any. They asked then, with an oath, what we did for a light. She replied that we burned kerosene in a lamp. Then they called for a lamp, and my wife had to get it, but the men in their eagerness to light it, turned the wick down in the oil. Failing to light it themselves, they called on my wife to light it.

" 'Why, you've ruined the lamp,' said she; 'it can't be lighted with the wick down in the oil.'

"Haven't you another lamp?" say they.

"Yes, there's one up stairs," said she, and they then ordered her to go and get it.

" 'Gentlemen,' said she, 'I can't do it. Your rudeness has so frightened me that I can scarcely hold my babe.'

"One of the men then offered to hold it for her, and took it from her arms. My poor wife then went and got the lamp, which they lighted and started on their search. They all cocked their revolvers and passed the word to kill me at sight, and started for the cellar. I laid myself as flat as I could, and turned my face toward the wall, for I knew my face was thinnest from ear to ear. The light came to the door.

"I tell you, brethren, I just quit living. You have heard it said that when a man is drowning all his past life comes up before him."

The speaker's voice trembled; his eyes became suffused, and his whole frame shook with suppressed emotion as he continued: "I stood then before the judgment seat. I was a dead man. My heart ceased to beat. I already stood before my Judge. Brethren, what could I do, but just trust myself to the Lord.

"The man who carried the light was tall, and providentially stooped so low in entering the cellar that the light shining against the bank of earth threw a shadow over me. They searched the cellar, but did not find me, and went back up stairs. My wife afterwards told me that when the men went down in the cellar, she took her babe and went into the parlor, and stood there holding her hand against one ear, and her babe against the other, expecting every moment to hear the report of the revolvers in the cellar, announcing the death of her husband.

(*139*)

"The soldiers set fire to the house in several places, and leaving one of their number to prevent my wife from putting it out, departed. The man seemed to be touched with pity, and told her that if she wanted to save some furniture he would help her. My wife thinks that holding the babe in his arms touched his heart. She pleaded with him if he had any consideration for her helpless children to leave the house and let her put out the fire. He consented and left.

"My wife then came to me and asked me whether it was all right between me and God. I am afraid they will come back and kill you yet, and it will be the greatest comfort to know that you felt prepared to die.

"I told her that I felt that I was prepared to die.

"Telling me to pray, she left me. It was not long before another party of Quantrell's men came, and in drunken tones—for the marauders had become intoxicated by this time—demanded whether I was in the house.

" 'Do you suppose,' said my wife, confidently, 'that he would stay here and you shooting and burning all over town? No; he left this morning as soon as the firing commenced, and unless some of you have shot him and killed him outside, he is safe. Some of your men were here this morning and searched the house. However, you may look for yourselves.'

"In this way she bluffed them. They set fire to the house, and left one, who drew his revolver on my wife, and said he would kill her if she tried to put it out. He stayed till the house was so far consumed that there was no possibility of saving it. My wife pulled up a carpet, and, taking it to the yard, dropped it accidentally by the door.

"My wife was afraid, and so was I, that I would be burned alive, for I had now no thought of doing anything but what my wife told me. The floor was on fire almost over me, and the flames were creeping nearer. My wife stood and threw water, pail after pail, on the floor, and was doing this when a neighbor, a Catholic woman, came and said: 'Why, Mrs. Fisher, what are you doing? What good will it be to save that floor? Besides, you can't save it.'

" 'I don't care what good it will do,' replied my wife, 'I am going to keep on wetting that floor.'

"But, finally, when she saw she could not save it, she asked the neighbor whether she could keep a secret. She then swore her by the Virgin Mary never to reveal it.

" 'Well, then,' said my wife, 'my husband is under that floor.'

"The soldiers were still everywhere, shooting and burning, and the air was filled with the shrieks of wounded and dying men, the wailings of widows and orphans, and the sound of falling buildings. My wife then called me to come out, and threw a dress over my shoulders. The two women picked up the carpet, and I crawled under it between them, and so we proceeded to a small bush about four feet high, out in the yard.

"There my wife saw four soldiers ready to fire. They were not a hundred yards off. Then, for the first time, the poor woman despaired. A pang then shot to her heart, and she gave up all for lost. Nevertheless, I slunk under the bush, and they threw the carpet over me.

" 'Save the chairs!' cried my wife; and they rushed to where the chairs were piled, close to the burning building, and ran with them and flung them carelessly upon me, and piled up all that was saved of our household goods about me. The soldiers, evidently, thought the pile only a lot of household furniture, and left it unmolested.

"I staid there till two hours after they left, and then gathered my wife and my four children—for the two boys had come back —and in the garden we knelt and thanked God for deliverance. Brethren, you don't know what it is to be thankful."

The Baxter Springs Affair.

Shortly after the Lawrence, Kansas, raid, Quantrell gathered his men together and went South, but on the way down determined to give the Federal forces stationed at Baxter Springs, Kansas, a slight "shake up." Accordingly, in October, 1863, they started on their southern trip, by

Jim Younger

way of Baxter Springs, which place they found strongly guarded and fortified. After slipping up within shooting distance a few rounds were fired and then a retreat was ordered. They were not pursued, and it was thought the Federals stationed there feared a trap was set for them.

Fight with Gen. Blunt's Bodyguard.

The next day, while on the road south, Quantrell met Gen. Blunt and his bodyguard, coming up. When Blunt saw Quantrell and his men he took them for Federals, and his brass band at once struck up a lively tune. Quantrell at once formed his men in line of battle, yet Blunt supposed they were forming to fire a salute. Blunt marched on up the road, not anticipating danger, and when they arrived within short range, Quantrell ordered his men to fire on them, which they did with murderous effect, killing nearly all of his men, about 80 in number, with a few exceptions. Gen. Blunt was one of the lucky ones. Blunt was riding in a buggy, and as soon as the firing commenced he jumped out, mounted a fleet horse, which was tied behind the buggy, with saddle and bridle on, and rode rapidly off. Quantrell captured Blunt's buggy and fine match horses, ambulance, brass band instruments, his sword, which was carried South and presented to Gen. Price; also a lot of arms, horses, &c. The men composing the band were about the only ones who made resistance, and they fought to the last. One of Younger's men got killed in charging the band wagon. Quantrell then went south and reported to Gen. Joe. Shelby, and the forces under his command were sent to the Mississippi river. Cole Younger remained here for some time and finally went to California.

(*143*)

Coleman and John Younger.

The Consollas Affair.

In the summer of 1868, two of the Younger Brothers, Coleman and John, were in Sedalia, Missouri. While there they chanced to meet upon the public road a man by the name of Consollas, who lived near Browning-ton, Henry county, Missouri. While in Sedalia, Consollas bantered the Younger boys for a game of cards, but they declined, stating that they seldom indulged in that kind of amusement, and when they did, it was simply for amuse-ment, and not for money. Consollas kept at them to play, and Cole told him if nothing else would do him, he would play him a few games of draw poker. After playing a short time Consollas' money began rapidly to pass from his possession into that of Younger's. After playing several hours Younger won all the money he had, $150. When the old man discovered that his money was all gone he began to get a little crusty and told Younger he believed he stole cards. "I did not," replied Younger. The old man replied, "I'll be d—d if you didn't." "You are mistaken," replied Cole Younger, "it was a fair game, but luck was against you, that is all. A man can't be in luck all the time." "Well," replied Consollas, "you have got my last dollar." "How far are you from home?" asked Younger. "Fifty miles," replied Consollas. "Well," replied Younger, "I will give you money enough to take you back to the old woman." "By G—d, I don't want to see the old woman in my fix; not a dollar in my pocket," replied the old man. "Well, I will give you a chance to win back your money," said Younger, "if you will get a stake from some of your friends.'. "What would be the use, d—n you, you would steal that, too." The language of the old man then got a little too insulting for Cole, and he slapped him in the face, and stepped out of the room.

A week or two after the above occurrence Cole Younger and two of his brothers, James and John, in company with a few friends, who had their families with them, started to move to Texas, his friends and their families stopping a few days at the Monegaw Springs, St. Clair county. Cole Younger and his brothers were yet in Lafayette county, but in a few days passed on down to Monegaw Springs. They passed through Clinton and Brownington, Henry county, on the road to the Monegaw Springs, close by the house of Consollas, where he kept store. Consollas recognized Cole Younger, and as soon as he and his brothers passed, Consollas set about to concoct some plan by which he could wreak vengeance upon him for the loss of his money as well as the slapping of his face. He had a large pasture, part prairie and part timber, and at once jumped upon a horse and went to his neighbors and told them that a certain gray horse was stolen out of the pasture, and from where the fence was thrown down, as from the traces he could see, he believed the thief had gone to Monegaw Springs. By these false representations he induced some ten or fifteen of his neighbors to accompany him to the Springs, he leading the party, well knowing who it was he wanted. Seeing them pass, and knowing the direction they took, he was not long in getting on the trail of the Younger Brothers, who had got with and met their moving friends at Monegaw Springs, according to promise. This was about the first of September, 1868. The weather was warm, and a great many persons were at the Springs, partaking of those healing waters, as well as enjoying the delightful breeze. Consollas and his party came upon the ground heavily armed with shot-guns and revolvers, seemingly on the war trail. Cole Younger eyed them closely and soon recognized the man he had won $150 of in Sedalia, and at once came to the conclusion that the old fellow was after nothing good. He watched him closely. Finally, Consollas and party moved about among the campers and told them of his having had a gray horse stolen in Henry county, and he believed them fellers, pointing to Cole Younger and his brothers, were the guilty parties, and asked them if they would assist to arrest them. Some of the men talked to, knew Cole Younger and his brothers, and they at once notified them of the business of the armed men. When Consollas was asked if his horse was upon the ground, he replied no, they had sold him. After learning these facts, Cole and his brothers, not desiring to have any difficulty, quietly mounted their horses and rode over the creek until they got out of sight of the armed mob, when they halted and grazed their horses. After the mob found that the Youngers had friends there, who did not believe them guilty of stealing horses, and finding that they were gone, they returned to their homes. It was afterwards proven that the old man had not lost a horse, and that his animal was in the pasture at that very time. After his neighbors who were fooled into the pretended hunt for horse thieves learned the facts in the case, they talked strongly of taking the old man out and flogging him. This circumstance is but one among many which have been gotten up to prejudice the public mind against the Youngers.

James H. Younger.

James H. Younger is near 29 years of age. He joined the forces of Quantrell in the year 1863, sometime after Coleman, and the cause of him doing so, was owing to the treatment his father and mother had received at the hands of the Jayhawkers, as well as the treatment he received at their hands on several occasions, although a mere boy. He is a young man of limited education, never having had an opportunity to avail himself of the means of getting one, owing to the troubled condition of the country, the bad feeling that existed shortly after the war, and to the fact that almost immediately on his return home after the war, he was compelled to move from place to place to prevent his personal enemies from taking his life. He was also kept in the military prison, in Kentucky, for about six months after the surrender of the Confederate forces.

During the war he figured less conspicuously than did his elder brother, Coleman, although we have been able to gather a few instances in which he showed great bravery and performed some almost miraculous feats.

A Narrow Escape in Kansas City.

In the summer of 1863, James Younger and four of his comrades went to Kansas City one night, which place was then held by the Federals. They rode their horses, managing to evade the pickets. After entering the city and hitching their horses in a back alley, they promenaded over town for some time, until finally the police found them out and gave them chase. They at once made for the bank of the river, hoping to find a skiff and make their escape across the river, for they at once saw plainly that they were cut off from their horses. James Younger was pressed so closely that he was compelled to run through an alley, thus cutting him off from the rest of the men. He continued his flight in the direction of the river, which point he gained in safety, but not finding a skiff, and hearing the near approach of his pursuers, had no time to conjecture or plan for escape, but at once jumped into the river with all of his clothes on, hoping to gain a sand bar in the river, distant about 300 yards. He had often seen this bar in the days of peace, long before war had cursed the land of his birth. He landed upon the bar in safety, where some driftwood had lodged. While swimming to the bar the policemen had sent bullets after him, but without taking effect. While pulling off his clothes preparatory to swimming across the river, he saw a steamboat coming up, and waited until it passed him. As it passed he concealed himself as best he could. The boat ran so close to him that the light from it lit up the bar upon which he was very brightly. As soon as it had passed and the dark mantle of night was again thrown over all around him, he pulled off his clothes and set out for the opposite shore, which he reached in safety. Believing that all of his comrades were on that side of the river, and feeling greatly exhausted, he at once commenced hooting like an owl, a very common practice with

Quantrell's men when out at night and wishing to find one another. This hoot was soon answered by four others, when he at once knew that his companions were near him. They were now in Clay county, Missouri, and he was naked, on foot and without arms. He at once climbed up the bank and hooted again, which was answered, and he and his companions were soon together again. After detailing to one another their escape, &c., James said to the others, "Boys, I must have a suit of clothes." "Well," replied James, "Liberty has got plenty in it." "Yes," one replied, "but how are you going to get there." "That don't make any difference," said James, "I must have them, and will. We have all lost our horses and must have a complete cavalry outfit to-night, and be upon the other side of the river before day lights up the Eastern horizon." "Well, that is the right kind of talk," was the reply. "Now, boys, we must get all we want from the Federals at Liberty," said Younger. "When we get within one mile of town we will leave the main road. By so doing we will miss the pickets. We will then follow the byroads and paths until we get near the camp guard, if they chance to have any out, but as it is a rainy night, they may not have any. Should they have them posted around the camp, we will skylight them or find their whereabouts, somehow." So on they went until they could discern the town through the darkness, by the white houses. Here they turned to the left and went into town in the rear. As they cautiously approached the camp James Younger stopped. He had seen a guard between him and a smoldering light. He then told his companions to squat down, and he would see where the next sentinel was placed upon post. Younger soon returned with the information that there was one other guard on that side of the town, and said he felt sure they could pass between the two, and if they could, they were all right, as it was now about one or two o'clock, and he thought the entire camp was asleep. Younger led the way to a small ditch, which run back from an alley, up this ditch and through the alley they went, passing the guards unobserved, and entering the Federal camp. Everything was as still as death—none were awake. There was no time to be lost. Younger soon got himself a suit of clothes. The next thing they needed was horses and equipments. They then went to where the horses were tied, selected the best ones they could find, procured saddles and bridles, put them on, and all was now ready to mount and leave, when Younger happened to think that he had no arms. He concluded that he would yet secure a couple of good revolvers, and at once crawled among the sleeping soldiers to secure pistols. This was soon done. After buckling on the revolvers he returned to his companions, who were waiting for him, when they mounted the horses and started to ride off. As they did so the cry sounded in their ears, "thieves in camp." It was now time to be getting away, and they put spurs to their horses and left on a double quick, making their way out about the same way they went in, running over the first picket they discovered going in, who was asleep, and made their way out in safety. The next thing was to cross the Missouri river before day. They arrived upon the river bank just as day was breaking, at an old crossing below Independence, where they plunged their horses into the river and swam safely over to the opposite shore, just as the lark had commenced to warble his morning notes.

(*152*)

Captured in Kentucky.

In the fall of 1864 James Younger accompanied Quantrell to Kentucky, the latter intending to go to his old home in Maryland. Quantrell then passed himself and his men off as Federals, drawing rations from the Federal officers at Louisville. One day, however, one of his men got drunk and yelled out in a loud voice for Quantrell, which at once aroused suspicion, and Quantrell learning the fact, drew his men off and a fight soon commenced, Quantrell cutting the telegraph wires and cutting up Jack generally. This discovery created much commotion in Federal circles throughout the State of Kentucky, the Federal officers scarcely knew what to do. During the battle with Quantrell and his men, in which the former was killed, or at least mortally wounded, James Younger was taken prisoner and sent to the Alton, Illinois, Military prison, remaining there until the summer of 1866, when he was released and returned home to Jackson county, Missouri, the home of his mother, where he and the other boys commenced to make rails and improve the farm, nearly everything having been destroyed during the war. But he was not long allowed to remain home in peace, as the Jayhawkers were continually visiting the home of their mother, in the hope of capturing Cole and James, the two oldest, who had been with Quantrell.

John Younger.

John Younger was 24 years of age at the time of his death.

John Younger, in 1865, in Independence, Mo., shot and killed a man. He was arrested and tried by the authorities and acquitted on the ground of self-defence, he being only 15 years of age at the time.

The nerve of the Youngers under circumstances the most disadvantageous, is one of their peculiar traits. They seem not to know what it is to be overpowered. No better illustration of the character of the Youngers need be cited than the shooting of John Younger by Capt. Lull, one of Pinkerton's Chicago detectives, in March, 1874, near Monegaw Springs, St. Clair county, Missouri. John Younger was sitting on his horse at the time, with his gun resting on the pommel of his saddle. Lull watched his opportunity, drew his revolver and shot John Younger full in the throat, tearing open the jugular vein. With the life-blood pouring in a great gushing stream, Younger actually straightened himself in his saddle, threw forward his gun, and, with deliberate aim, poured a heavy load of buckshot into Capt. Lull's chest and left arm, and then dropped his gun and drew his revolver, which he emptied into the body of Lull and Ed. Daniels, before he fell from his horse. With truth it may be said that there are few instances of like character on record.

But this was not the first time that John Younger had shown that strange characteristic of the genuine border desperado; the almost superhuman faculty of looking unflinchingly into the face of death, and struggling up from a blow which would have crushed 999 men out of every 1,000, to inflict a mortal wound upon his slayer. He was not out of his teens when the war closed. The mother, broken down by the unceasing persecutions of the Jayhawkers, had gathered her children about her on the farm they had been forced to abandon in Jackson county at the outbreak of the war. John Younger had returned, and Cole and Jim, the eldest brothers, were supposed to have come back also. It was asking too much of human nature to think the memories of the border actrocities could be wiped out by the surrender at Appomattox.

The Jayhawkers Hang John Up.

One night a band of Jayhawkers swooped down on the farm house, broke in the doors and windows, and, with ready revolvers in hand, sprang in to wipe out a long score with the Guerrillas. They found only the poor woman dying with consumption, her children about her. Disappointed at not meeting the older brothers, they took John Younger to the barn. They had reason to believe that Cole and Jim were still in the vicinity. A rope was thrown over a beam, the noose put around the boy's neck, and he was told that only by revealing the hiding place of his brothers could he save his life. Three times he was strung up until almost dead, then lowered and resuscitated, but only refused to give the desired information. The fourth time the furious band left him dangling in the air until the rope had cut through the skin and buried itself in the boy's neck. When the rope was lowered he lay limp and lifeless on the stable-floor without perceptible respiration. It was half an hour before consciousness began to return, and when, weak and panting, their victim was unable to stand, the fiends wounded him with their sabres, forced him to accompany them, accelerating his speed from time to time by striking him upon the shoulders with the butts of their muskets. The next morning he crawled back home half dead, to find his mother's end hastened by the agonizing suspense of the night. Soon after that the mother of the Youngers died, and the boys become wanderers without a local habitation beyond the wild cattle ranches of Western Texas. Much of their time was spent on the cattle trail from the Mexican border to Missouri.

Killing of the Sheriff at Dallas, Texas.

About the first of January, 1871, John Younger stopped for a short time in Dallas, Texas, and was engaged in clerking in a store. While there he met an old Missourian, named Nichols, who was then sheriff of the county. Nichols had been a Colonel in the Confederate army. Several accounts have been published in newspapers of the origin and termination of the difficulty he had there, but we are informed on reliable authority that the accounts thus published were incorrect, in the main facts, in regard to the case, and we shall proceed to give the true version of the difficulty, as we learn it from one who was a friend to both parties.

One night John Younger and a friend were in a saloon, and all had been indulging pretty freely, and joking and sport was carried on to a considerable extent. There was in the saloon at the time an old codger who was generally regarded as a fool, and with whom almost everybody took greater or less liberty. After some joking with him, John Younger told him to stand still and he would show him how close he could shoot to his nose without hitting it. John Younger then drew his revolver and fired several shots, each time the ball passing very close to the old man's nose. At length Younger put up his revolver and let the old man alone, as he observed that he seemed very much frightened.

Some of the crowd then got around the old man and made him believe that Younger was trying to kill him, and advised him to go and swear out a States warrant for Younger. The old man finally left the saloon and actually did go and swear out a warrant for the arrest of Younger. After remaining in the saloon for some time Younger went to the hotel and then to bed. As before stated, a warrant was issued that night and placed in the hands of the Sheriff, who went to the hotel early the next morning in search of Younger, and found him in bed. He told Younger that he had a warrant for his arrest, when Younger replied, "All right; give me time to get my breakfast, and I will report at your office in an hour." The Youngers were well known, all along the border, at that time, and the Sheriff, apparently acquiesced in the arrrangement and went off. Younger calmly and cooly dressed himself, ate his breakfast, and walked to the stable to look at his horse. A guard stood at the stable-door and refused him entrance. Infuriated at the apparent want of faith on the part of the Sheriff, Younger turned on his heel and strode into the Sheriff's office. An armed man stood at the door, and as Younger pushed in, another man, with a gun between his knees, grudgingly made room for him. Walking straight up to the Sheriff, Younger said: "You have not treated me right, Colonel." The Sheriff replied stiffly and drew his revolver. Younger at once followed the movement, and simultaneously came the fire. The Sheriff dropped dying, shot through the chest. Younger stepped back, and, as he did so, the man at the door raised his gun and poured a double charge of buckshot in Younger's left arm and shoulder, tearing the flesh into shreds. So close was the range that the flash of the powder cauterized the wound, in a measure. Younger went down under the fearful shock, but in a moment struggled to his feet, and, putting his revolver to the man's breast, shot him dead.

He then took a grey horse from a ranch near by, belonging to a neighborhood Doctor, and fled, in company with an old Confederate friend, aiming for Red River, which place he reached by sunrise the next morning, a distance of 80 miles. After reaching the north bank of the river, the Sheriff's party arrived on the opposite bank, in pursuit of Younger, when some shots were exchanged between the parties, two of the Sheriff's party being wounded. The Sheriff's party then retraced their steps. Younger and his friend took breakfast at the house of a friend near by. Here Younger had his wounds dressed for the first time. After breakfast and his wounds were dressed, he left for St. Clair county, Missouri, where he stopped with a friend, near Chalk Level, until about the first of June, 1871, when he went to Kansas City, took the cars for California, and in a few days reached the house of his uncle. He was not satisfied here, and after remaining but a few months, he started back to the States, by rail. After the train left a station 200 miles west of Denver, Colorado, he jumped off the cars. His jumping off was caused by a couple of Detectives getting on the cars at this station, and after sitting a moment, eyed Younger, as he supposed, and then told him to surrender, at the same time drawing a pistol. Younger then drew his pistol, and shot the Detective who spoke, and then jumped out of the window. As was afterwards learned, the Detective was not after Younger, but the man who was in the seat with him. Younger, after jumping from the train, made for the mountains. He was then 200 miles from Denver, amid the lofty peaks of the Rocky Mountains. He then steered his course the best he could in the direction of Denver City, and finally arrived at a friendly habitation, upon one of the small tributaries at the head of the Green River. By this time he was worn out by fatigue and exhaustion, his feet one blister. He was now 75 miles from Denver. Here he hired a ranchman to convey him on horseback to Denver City, for which conveyance he paid him $75, which took nearly all the money he had. He staid there but a few days, and when some teams were starting for Kansas, he succeeded in getting with them as teamster simply for his board. After getting into the interior of Kansas he left the teams and started across the country on foot, aiming to get to Independence, Mo., where he arrived at his uncle's, Dr. Twyman, who lives near Blue Mills, Jackson county, completely worn out. Not being accustomed to walking, the trip was very hard

(*160*)

Bob Younger

on him, as he was but 19 years of age, though he had seen
much trouble and knew how to endure it. From the name
the Youngers have, the reader would suppose he would
have stolen at least a mustang pony, but such was not the
case. After returning from this trip, he was asked why he
did not steal a pony, and he replied that he never wanted
the name of a horse thief; our names are bad enough now,
and I never want the name of horse thief added—I was
raised by honest and pious parents and could not think of
disgracing their untimely ashes by such an act. The cry
against me and my brothers is false to a great extent, and
for what we are guilty, rests upon other shoulders. (He
refers to the death of his parents, and says they cry us
down to have us murdered.) My life has never been any
satisfaction to me, but has been but one continued series of
troubles, etc. If I thought I would have to endure as much
trouble as I have done in the next ten years I would rather
die now. Money caused the death of Pa, and now the ras-
cals of the country, to get money, are robbing bank after
bank, and all is laid to the Youngers. One may be robbed
in Denver to-day and one in Louisville, Ky., and both will
be charged to the Youngers.

Robert Ewing Younger.

Robert Younger is the youngest of the boys, being now only 22 years of age. He was too young to take part in the late war, but, as he grew up to manhood and learned and saw the brutal treatment of his father and mother, necessarily became revengeful and entertained but little love for those who took part in it, or in any way sympathized with those who were participants in these outrages. We have but little of his life, singly, though much in connection with one or more of his brothers, which will be found under appropriate headings.

John and Robert E. Younger.

Charged with Stealing Horses.

About the first of December, 1873, a horse was stolen in Clay county, Missouri, and a certain man in the neighborhood who did not like the Youngers, at once accused the boys of taking the horse. He at length succeeded in making the loser of the animal believe that it could be found in St. Clair county, and asked that a party of men accompany him to where, he believed, the horse could be recovered. As the sequel afterwards proved, a party accompanied him as far as Appleton City, in St. Clair county, where additional recruits were added, when the whole party proceeded to the vicinity of Monegaw Springs, in St. Clair county, Missouri, the neighborhood in which the Youngers usually resort when in that section of country. A man by the name of Morrow was about to mount his horse and ride to a neighbor's, when he discovered a party of armed men coming towards him. Mr. Morrow become somewhat alarmed at the sight of armed men, not knowing what it meant, and proceeded to mount his horse. Seeing the movements of Mr. Morrow, and by this time being nearly in gun-shot range, the approaching mob called to him to halt, at the same time quickening their speed. Mr. Morrow owned a very fine horse, and, as was afterwards learned, it answered, at a distance, very well the description of the one stolen in Clay county. As soon as Mr. Morrow was commanded to "halt," he put spurs to his horse and rode rapidly away. He was pursued, but his pursuers were soon left far in the rear. John and Robert Younger happened to be in the neighborhood at the time, and a friend of theirs chanced to meet the armed mob, who inquired of him for certain ones of the Youngers, at the same time stating that one of the Youngers was riding a horse that had been stolen in Clay county, Missouri, and, further, that they were out on the hunt for the Youngers. Learning that a party was in search of them, the Youngers started on the war trail, in search of the hunting party. The six doubly armed men extended their search as far as Roscoe, also in St. Clair county, which place they reached on the morning of the 8th of December, 1873. They next scoured the Osage hills, going in the direction of Chalk Level, which lies northwest of the Monegaw Springs, but after traveling the Chalk Level road some three miles, four of the party filed to the left, in the direction of Monegaw Springs. The Younger boys being in search of the hunting party all this time, at length came upon and captured the four at Monegaw Springs.

They Disarm Their Pursuers.

The Youngers, after disarming their prisoners, took them to the Monegaw Hotel and had a good breakfast prepared for them, but the poor fellows had lost their appetites, and all, save one, ate sparingly, while he, poor creature, could not eat anything—he was sick—sick at heart, and longed to be with his wife and children. After breakfast was over Robert Younger formed the prisoners in line and made them a speech, the substance of which was as follows:

SPEECH OF ROBERT YOUNGER.

"Now, gentlemen, we have you in our power, and can do with you as we wish, and I feel satisfied that were our positions changed, were we at your mercy, beyond a doubt you would kill both of us. But we are men—men possessing too much brave blood to be guilty of such cruel and cowardly butchery. There were and still are certain parties whose political views differed from ours at the breaking out of the late war, and certain men of the opposite party murdered and robbed our old father, who was a Union man, and a peaceable and quiet citizen, all for the sake of a few hundred dollars. The most damnable act of all, however, was the stripping of our widowed mother of all her stock and provision of every kind, and compelling her to fire her own house with her own hands, destroying all the clothing of herself and little children, and thus turning her out, penniless, and without sufficient clothing, upon the cold charities of the world, during the cold blasts of winter, the snow at the time six inches deep on the ground. She was thus compelled to call upon friends and strangers for assistance—for clothing sufficient to keep herself and children from freezing. She was afterwards driven from place to place, and finally brought to an untimely grave, caused by exposure and the wretched and inhuman treatment she received at the hands of Jayhawkers and Home Guards, under the sanction of the Federal authorities. Humanity shudders at the thought. What think you, gentlemen, must be our feelings when reflecting over these things? Some of you, if not all, are members of that same political party which perpetrated these hellish acts of cruelty, not only on our father and mother, but on hundreds of others. And you, sirs, are still trying to implicate me and my brothers in every species of rascality and crime committed in Missouri, and also in other States.

"Now, gentlemen, we set you at liberty; go to your homes and stay there. We want to stay the hand of blood, if possible, and live in peace, but if we can't be permitted to live as peaceable citizens, the blame will rest upon other men's shoulders, not upon ours. You know that my brother Cole was accused of being one of the party who robbed the Iowa railroad train, which occurred July 21st, 1873. At that time, I and my brother Cole were in St. Clair county, Missouri, at these very Springs, probably in this very hotel. The robbery was committed on Monday morning, and on Sunday morning we were down in the bottom and attended preaching. This we can prove by some of the best citizens of the county, and by the minister who preached, Rev. Mr. Smith, of Greenton Valley Church, Lafayette county, Missouri, who was here at the time on a visit. After it was discovered that we could prove this charge false, then we were accused of being horse thieves, and it was insisted that we had been stealing horses. We can prove a good title to every horse we have had since the war, and yet the damn fool party who differs with us politically, has called upon Governor Woodson, of Missouri, to hunt us out of St. Clair county, and the State, as though we were a band of thieves and robbers. But I do hope that Governor Woodson possesses too much good sense and intelligence to believe the Radical lies told by men whose hands are still red with the blood of our dear old father, who was so brutally murdered. These scoundrels endeavor to cover up their own damnable acts by shouting 'murder' and 'thief,' at the backs of other people. And why? They would rejoice at the destruction of myself and brothers, simply because they fear vengeance at our hands, a just retribution. We disclaim any such intention. All we ask, all we pray for, is to be left alone, to be allowed to enjoy ourselves in peace, and follow some useful and honorable avocation. The war has long since ceased, and as we know and believe there is a just God, who will punish all wrong-doers, with him we are willing to let the matter rest.

"Now mount your horses, gentlemen, and go back to Appleton City, and stay there. We don't want to hurt any of you, and do not, by your rashness and folly, compel us to kill any of you, for the task is an unpleasant one; but, as sure as there is a God in Heaven, if we will not be allowed to live in peace, we are ready to

(*168*)

sell our lives as dearly as possible. We wish you a safe and pleasant journey home, but under no circumstances must you come back."

At the conclusion of the speech of Robert Younger, both the Youngers shook hands with the party, thus proving to them that they bore no ill-will towards them. The hunting party started out to capture the Youngers, dead or alive, if they could overhaul them, and their friends were confident that such would be the case. Their astonishment can be better imagined than described when they returned and the fact became known that the Youngers had captured them, and the kind treatment they had received at the hands of their captors. This circumstance did much to allay the feeling that many had previously entertained towards the Youngers.

James H. and John Younger.

In July, 1873, after the Iowa railroad robbery, some of the Younger boys having been charged with participation in the affair, an armed posse from Iowa and elsewhere arrived at Appleton City, St. Clair county, Mo., and immediately went to work to procure additional recruits to go to Monegaw Springs to capture the Youngers. By the time the party started in pursuit their number tallied about forty men, all well armed, and supposed to be brave and determined men, who knew no fear, and all that was necessary was merely to see a Younger, and he was sure to be their prisoner, dead or alive. The party divided into squads of ten each, and commenced scouring the country in search of somebody, they scarcely knew who, but as the Youngers had a bad name, they were sure to suffer if any of them could be found. The whole pretext for all this parade of armed men in St. Clair county, was caused by the fact of some newspaper having asserted that it was believed that some of the Younger boys had a hand in the affair, as they were known to be brave and resolute men, fearing no danger.

Jim and John Younger were in the neighborhood of the Springs at the time, and learning that a party of soldiers, as they had been termed, were on the hunt for them, at once mounted their horses and went to search for the soldiers. They finally overhauled seven of them in the road, and after halting them, inquired of them if they were on the hunt for Youngers. To this inquiry one of the men replied, "We are on the hunt for certain ones of the Youngers." On being told that they (Jim and John) represented the whole family, and that their names were those they wanted, and that they, the soldiers, should take them, the Youngers, if they could, the whole seven heavily armed soldiers commenced scattering through the timber in every direction. The Youngers are dead shots, and could have killed every one of them had they so desired. John Brown and his party, part of this same gang, went to the house of an old black man living near Monegaw Springs, and seeing a black mare in the lot near the house, which, at a distance, answered the description of the horse they were told Cole Younger rode, attempted to take it, whereupon the old black woman made war upon them and drove them out of the lot, asking them if they did not know a mare from a horse.

Again Pursued to St. Clair County.

About the first of March, a train on the Iron Mountain Railroad was flagged and robbed, and in a day or two afterwards detectives were sent to St. Clair county, Missouri, where the Youngers were staying, to hunt them up and implicate them in the affair, as it was known that James and John were then staying in St. Clair county. One of the Detectives, who went by the name of Wright, but whose real name is Boyle, a native of Maryland, and who had been in the Confederate army during the war, remained in and around Osceola for a week or ten days previous to the raid upon the Youngers. Boyle, alias Wright, told the author of this book himself that he had been with the Youngers, James and John, but a day or two previous, at Chalk Level, distant from Monegaw Springs five miles. The termination of the affair proved that Wright was not alone in this matter, but that one of Pinkerton's Chicago Detectives, and one of his very best, shrewdest and bravest men, was also in the county, who went by the name of Allen, but whose real name was Lull. During the stay of Wright in Osceola he made the acquaintance of a young man of the town named Edwin B. Daniels, who sometimes acted as Deputy Sheriff, a man of considerable nerve and courage, highly respected in the county, and who, as it afterwards became known, acted as a guide, and probably agreed to help capture the Youngers, he being well acquainted with them, and was, doubtless, promised a liberal share of the reward offered for their capture.

On Monday morning, the 15th of March, 1874, Daniels and Wright left Osceola for Roscoe, as they stated, to look after cattle. Allen joined them somewhere, or probably left Osceola with them. After reaching Roscoe, twelve miles distant, in St. Clair county, the three men whiled away the remainder of the day and night in the town, staying all night in the Roscoe House. Early the next morning, after breakfast, they all left Roscoe and went in the direction of Chalk Level, the road to which passes the house of Mr. Theodrick Snuffer, one of the oldest residents in the county, having lived where he now resides about forty years, and whose character and standing in the community is beyond

(*173*)

reproach. Mr. Snuffer is a distant relative of the Youngers, and whether the boys are guilty of any crimes or not, old man Snuffer does not believe so, but thinks that their persecution grew out of the fact that they were what is generally called "Rebels." Very frequently when the boys are in the county they stop a day or night with the old gentleman, who is very old and feeble. Wright, being a Marylander, and knowing Mr. L. H. Brown, residing on the Chalk Level and Roscoe road, about one mile from Roscoe, stopped to converse with him, while Daniels and Allen went on. Wright did not overtake Allen and Daniels until they had passed the house of Mr. Snuffer, which is three miles north of Roscoe. Allen and Wright stopped at the fence in front of Mr. Snuffer's house, made inquiry about the road to the widow Sims' house and had some little conversation with old man Snuffer, after which they rode on, but did not take the road they were directed to travel. James and John Younger were in Mr. Snuffer's house at the time eating dinner. The movements of the two men were closely watched by both the Youngers, without being discovered, and when it was observed that they did not take the road they were directed to travel, and noticing that Allen and his horse were strangers in the county, the suspicions of the Youngers were at once aroused and a consultation was had.

The Fight with Detectives.

At length they both agreed that the men were detectives, and on the hunt for them, so they determined to mount their horses and follow them, and, if possible, ascertain who they were and what their business was. After Allen and Daniels had passed the house about two or three hundred yards, they were joined by Wright, who, by this time, had overtaken them. We have not been able to ascertain, definitely, where Daniels and the two detectives were about one hour, after passing the house of Mr. Snuffer, as about that time elapsed before the Youngers met them and the fight commenced, but the circumstances go to show that they were at a negro cabin, near by, probably trying to get some information about the Youngers.

The first news received in Osceola of the fight, was brought by Wright, who said he managed to escape, but thought that Allen and Daniels had both been killed. The story of Wright, as related to us at the time, agrees with that of Allen up to the time Wright left, with the exception that he, Wright, says he was behind Allen and Daniels, instead of in front, as Allen says in his testimony before the Coroner's Jury. At the time we interviewed Allen at Roscoe, we mentioned the fact to him that Wright had stated to us that he, Wright, was behind when fired on, and asked him, Allen, if he might not be mistaken in this matter, as in every particular their testimony agreed, up to to the time Wright left, with that exception. Allen, after studying a moment, said he might be mistaken. The following is the statement of Mr. Allen, before the Coroner's inquest:

KILLING OF JOHN YOUNGER AND ED. DANIELS.

W. J. Allen, being duly sworn, testified as follows: Yesterday about half-past two o'clock, the 16th of March, 1874, E. B. Daniels and myself were riding along the road from Roscoe to Chalk Level, which road runs past the house of one Theodrick Snuffer, and about three miles from the town of Roscoe, and in St. Clair county, Missouri, Daniels and myself were riding side by side, and Wright a short distance ahead of us; some noise behind us attracted our attention, and we looked back and saw two men on horseback coming towards us, and one was armed with a double-barrel shotgun, the other with revolvers; don't know if the other had a shot-gun or not; the one had the shotgun cocked, both barrels, and ordered us to halt; Wright drew his pistol and put spurs to his horse and rode off; they ordered him to halt, and shot at him and shot off his hat, but he kept on riding. Daniels and myself stopped, standing across the road on our horses; they rode up to us, and ordered us to take off our pistols and drop them in the road, the one with the gun covering me all the time with the gun. We dropped our pistols on the ground, and one of the men told the other to follow Wright and bring him back, but he refused to go, saying he would stay with him; one of the men picked up the revolvers we had dropped, and looking at them, remarked they were damn fine pistols, and they must make them a present of them; one of them asked me where we came from, and I said Osceola; he then wanted to know what we were doing in this part of the country; I replied, rambling around. One of them then said, you were up here one day before; I replied that we were not; he then said we had been at the Springs; I replied, we had been at the Springs, but had not been inquiring for them, that we did not know them, and they said detectives had been up there hunting for them all the time, and they were going to stop it. Daniels then said, I am no detective; I can show you who I am and where I belong; and one of them said he knew him, and then turned to me and said, what in the hell are you riding around here with all them pistols on for? and I said, good God! is not every man wearing them that is traveling, and have I not as much right to wear them as any one else? and the one that had the shot-gun said, hold on, young man, we don't want any of that, and then lowered the gun, cocked, in a threatening manner; then Daniels had some talk with them, and one of them got off his horse and picked up the pistols; two of them were mine and one was Daniels'; the one mounted had the gun drawn on me, and I concluded that they intended to kill us. I reached my hand behind me and drew a No. 2

(*176*)

Smith & Wesson pistol and cocked it and fired at the one on horseback, and my horse frightened at the report of the pistol and turned to run, and I heard two shots and my left arm fell, and then I had no control over my horse, and he jumped into the bushes and the trees checked his speed, and I tried to get hold of the rein with my right hand, to bring him into the road; one of the men rode by me and fired two shots at me, one of which took effect in my left side, and I lost all control of my horse and he turned into the brush, and a small tree struck me and knocked me out of the saddle. I then got up and staggered across the road and lay down until I was found. No one else was present.

W. J. ALLEN.

Subscribed and sworn to, before me, this 18th day of March, 1874.

JAMES ST. CLAIR.

James Younger, however, gives quite a different version of the commencement of the shooting, as told by him to old man Snuffer, a few moments afterwards, and also the same evening, to an intimate friend of his, who happened to fall in with him before he, James Younger, left the country. James says that after leaving the house of Mr. Snuffer they took the near cut, coming out on the Chalk Level road about half a mile from the house, and as they came to a turn in the road they met the three men, apparently coming down from the negro house. He says they were about passing them, and had "bid them the time of the day," when the man on the white horse, which was Allen, drew his revolver and shot John Younger in the neck, and that immediately afterwards Daniels drew his revolver and fired at him, Jim Younger, and that he threw himself on the right side of his horse to avoid the shot taking effect in his body, and that in so doing he fell from his horse, and that his horse became frightened and got away from him. Jim Younger also asserts that John fired at the man on

(*177*)

the white horse with his double-barrel shotgun as soon as Allen shot him, and then drew his revolver, dropping the gun, and shot Ed. Daniels, and then went in pursuit of Allen, who was fleeing through the timber, shooting him, Allen, several times, until he, John Younger, fell dead from his horse.

The following additional evidence was taken at the coroner's inquest:

"I heard a shot a couple of hundred yards from my house, and I found out after the first shot that it was John and James Younger; after the first shot they ceased firing for some time, and then commenced again, but I had not seen any of the parties; but after several shots had been fired, another man, who I did not know, come down the road, and I think they were both shooting at one another; I am certain that John Younger was shooting at the other man; he continued to run down the road east of here; I think Younger passed the man on the gray horse; about the time John Younger passed him I saw him sink on his horse, as if going to fall; don't know what become of him afterwards; then Younger turned to come west and began to sink, and then fell off his horse; then James Younger come down by here on foot, to where John Younger was lying, and the horse that John Younger was riding, and that was the last I saw of James Younger.

JOHN McFARREN.

Subscribed and sworn to before me, this 18th day of March, 1874.

JAMES ST. CLAIR, J. P.

The testimony of John R. McFarren was corroborative of that of John McFarren, both of whom were together.

Two men came to my house and inquired the way to Mrs. Sims'; the third man came along afterwards and overtook them; the two Youngers, John and James, after they had passed, followed them; I saw James Younger after the fight; he told me that John Younger was dead; that they had killed one of the men and that one other

(*178*)

had been wounded, Allen; that Allen had a pistol secreted and fired the first shot.   THEODRICK SNUFFER.

Subscribed and sworn to before me, this 18th day of March, 1874.

JAMES ST. CLAIR, J. P.

John Younger fell from his horse; James Younger came running up to where John had fallen and called me to him; he then turned him (John Younger) over and took some revolvers off of him and a watch and something else out of his pockets; I do not know what else; I saw John Younger and another man shooting at each other, when the first firing commenced; I think James Younger took four revolvers off of John Younger, his brother; he threw one over the fence and told me to keep it; he then told me to catch a horse and go down and tell Snuffer's folks.

G. W. McDONALD.

Sworn to and subscribed before me, this 18th day of March, 1874.

JAMES ST. CLAIR, J. P.

All we know concerning the death of the two men, being the same that the inquest is being held over, is that the one, John Younger, come to his death from the effects of a gun-shot wound, which entered the right side of his neck, touching the clavical bone, on the upper side, and about two inches from the meridian, went nearly straight through the neck; the orifice is small, indicating that he was shot with a small ball. The other man, Edwin B. Daniels, came to his death from the effects of a gunshot wound, which entered the left side of the neck, about one inch from the meridian line, and about midway of the neck, opposite the aesophagus, and as per examination, went nearly straight through the neck, striking the bone; the orifice was pretty large, indicating that the ball was of a pretty large size.   A. C. MARQUIS, M. D.

L. LEWIS, M. D.

Subscribed and sworn to before me, this 18th day of March, 1874.

JAMES ST. CLAIR, J. P.

The following names comprise the Coroner's jury, with A. Ray as foreman: A. Ray, G. W. Cox, J. Davis, W. Holmes, R. C. Gill and H. Gleason.

(*179*)

The verdict of the jury was as follows:

We, the jury, find that John Younger came to his death by a pistol shot, supposed to have been in the hands of W. J. Allen.

A. RAY, Foreman.

We, the jury, find that Ed. B. Daniels came to his death by a pistol shot, supposed to have been fired by the hand of James Younger.

A. RAY, Foreman.

We have given all the evidence procurable in the case, of both parties, in order that the public might judge for themselves and form their own conclusion.

James Younger received a flesh wound in the left side, above the hip, supposed to have been done by Ed. Daniels. John Younger was buried at a family burying ground, on the Osceola and Chalk Level road, about three miles west of Osceola. The body of Ed. Daniels was taken charge of by friends and brought to Osceola, where it was decently interred, in the Osceola Cemetery, and his remains were followed to their last resting place by almost the entire community, who universally respected the deceased. Capt. Lull, alias Allen, suffered for about six weeks before he died. During his sickness he was at the Roscoe House, Roscoe, where every attention was given him, and he had the best medical attendance in the county, if not in Southwest Missouri, having been attended by Dr. D. C. McNeil, of Osceola, an old and experienced army surgeon. In his last moments he was surrounded by his wife and brother, who came on to Roscoe from Chicago. His remains were placed in a metallic coffin and taken to Chicago, where he was buried with Masonic honors. This sad and fatal occurrence cast a gloom over the entire county, all regretting

(*180*)

that the detectives had paid the county a visit, as it was well known to many that both James and John Younger were in the county at the time the railroad train was flagged and robbed.

Coleman, James and Robert Younger.

After the fight between the Chicago Detectives, near the farm of Mr. Theodrick Snuffer, St. Clair county, Missouri, and John and James Younger, and John was killed, in March, 1874, James Younger went to Boone county, Arkansas.

In June, 1874, Cole Younger, who was then in Mississippi, Robert being with him, happened to get hold of a newspaper containing an account of the battle and the death of John Younger. Cole and Robert immediately thereafter mounted their horses and struck out through the country for Arkansas, with the hope of finding James in Boone county, at the house of a friend, a place he and they were in the habit of visiting, and learning all the particulars of the fight, the death of John, etc. They at length reached the place of their destination, and were not disappointed in their expectations, as they found James, who narrated to them all the circumstances attending the battle, as well as the death and burial of John.

A Night Attack.

After remaining here a few days, one night Cole and Bob went to the house of a neighbor, leaving James at the

(*183*)

house of their friend. About the break of day the next morning firing was heard in the direction of the house at which James was stopping, which they had left the evening previous. At the time they were at a loss to know the cause, but at once proceeded to mount their horses and ride over to the house, arriving only in time to get a glimpse of the retreating party. It was afterwards learned that some horses had been stolen in the neighborhood a day or two previous, and as some strange men were seen going to the house, suspicion rested upon them in the minds of the citizens, which led to the attack upon the house. James at once became alarmed at seeing a mob around the house at such an early hour in the morning. He slipped up stairs, and going to the window to ascertain, if possible, the cause of the trouble, he was at once fired upon by those in front of the house. He immediately returned the fire, killing one man, and wounding another. After this the mob fled.

Attacked While Watering Their Horses.

The Younger Brothers, after this fracas, mounted their horses and started for the home of a friend, living south of the Arkansas river. On the second day, while watering their at a creek, a party of twelve men rode up in sight of them and commenced firing on them. They at once returned the fire. Cole's horse was shot dead under him, but, after dismounting, he kept up a fire on the enemy on foot until the pursuing party fled. None of the boys were wounded in this engagement, although several of the pursuing party were.

Another Attack.

The boys then continued to proceed on towards their destination. Cole purchased a horse the next morning. They crossed the Arkansas River at Roseville, twenty-five miles below Van Buren. After they had crossed the river a short distance, on the Thoroughfare road, they chanced to meet an old Confederate friend of Cole's, on his way to Louisiana. After proceeding on their journey some distance, the party stopped in a ravine, and Jim and Bob went up the ravine to a spring. It seems that horse stealing had been going on in this section also, a few days previous, and the excitement was up to fever heat, and that parties were scouring the country in almost every direction. Cole and his friend were sitting on their horses talking of war times, and waiting for Jim and Robert to return. Cole happened to look back on the road, and he discovered some twenty-five or thirty armed men coming towards them at a rapid rate. About the time he discovered the advancing party they also observed him, and at once commenced increasing the speed of their horses. When they had approached within about one hundred yards, they at once opened fire, which was returned by Cole Younger and his friend, without their knowing the cause. The fight was hotly contested for several moments. Five of the attacking party were killed during the fight and several wounded, but those who were wounded were taken off when they retreated. Cole was shot in the right knee with buckshot, and his horse was also badly wounded. Jim and Bob returned about the time the fight commenced, and took an active part in the engagement, firing on the enemy's right wing. Cole's horse, after

(*185*)

being wounded, dashed through the timber, and his head struck against a tree, which blinded him for a moment. Neither of the other Younger's nor Cole's friend were harmed.

After the enemy had retreated, the boys and their friend proceeded on their journey towards the place of their destination. They had not proceeded far, however, before Cole's horse, which had been wounded, gave out, and they were compelled to leave him on the road. Jim then dismounted and gave Cole his horse, walking with the party, until they could purchase another horse, which they succeeded in doing the next day.

They Return to Missouri.

They then determined to go to Missouri, to the house of a friend, where Cole could have his wound attended to. They recrossed the Arkansas River near Dardanelle, their friend proceeding on his journey to Louisiana. It was then determined to separate, Jim and Bob going one route and Cole another, agreeing to meet in Fulton county, Arkansas, at the house of a friend. The separation was agreed upon under the belief that they might be pursued, and it was thought best for Cole to go alone, in his wounded condition, thus lessening the probability, as they thought, of his being followed. Their surmises proved correct, as the sequel proved.

James and Robert Pursued.

While Jim and Bob were in the eastern part of Marion county, Arkansas, stopping for dinner, their horses grazing, Jim was lying down on the grass, asleep, while Bob

(*186*)

was sitting under the tree whittling, he heard some one sing out, "surrender, you damn thieves," and looking up, saw two men at the yard gate, some forty yards distant, with guns in their hands; one of the men standing directly in front of the gate, while the other was standing a few feet to the right, at the side of a wagon. The call awoke Jim and he sprang to his feet. As he rose both men at the yard fence fired, one of their shots taking effect in the neck of Jim. Almost at the same time Bob fired at the man by the side of the wagon, shooting him through the chest. Seeing other men coming towards the house, Bob and Jim made for the brush, leaving their horses in the pasture. Before reaching the brush they were further pursued and fired upon, another ball striking Jim in the right hip, passing through, and coming out at the lower part of the abdomen. Notwithstanding the two dangerous wounds Jim had received, he continued to flee and finally gained the brush, where they were able to elude their pursuers, who gave up the chase and turned their attention to their dead companion and the captured horses. Shortly after gaining the brush Jim fainted from loss of blood, but his brother Bob helped and urged him on to where they could procure water with which to bathe and dress his wounds.

This single circumstance is one of many which goes to show the pluck and determination of the Youngers, a characteristic of all of them, as none but an extraordinary man could have stood up and traveled about one mile before water was reached. On the route Jim fainted five or six times. After reaching water Bob took the shirt from his person, bathed and dressed the wounds of his brother, and then the two proceeded on their journey during the whole night, being guided by the stars as best they could. About an hour before sunrise the next morning they neared a large farm house, and Bob at once determined to secrete Jim in the brush and endeavor to purchase horses as soon as work was commenced on the farm.

Two Horses Pressed into Service.

After the lapse of about one hour, two young men were seen coming into a field to plow. Bob crossed over to where the nearest one to him was, and after bidding him the time of day, asked him if his father was at home, &c., and learning that the old gentleman was out after horse-thieves, about six miles distant, the place at which the fight took place the afternoon previous, told the young man that he wanted to buy his mare, (she having a colt,) and that he would give him all she was worth and allow him to keep the colt. The boy said he would see his brother, and the two went over to where the other young man was, and he was made acquainted with the facts and also told that he could sell his horse on the same terms. The boy at once flew into a rage, telling his brother to go to the house and get the gun, and they would shoot the damn thief. Younger insisted that he did not want to steal the horses, but would pay him the money for both, but the boy was not to be argued into selling them, and insisted on his brother going to the house for the gun to shoot the thief. Younger seeing that words and money were of no avail, and considering the helplessness of his brother, determined to have the horses at all hazards, so he drew his pistol and told both boys to unharness the horses and follow him, which they at once proceeded to do. They then went to where Jim was lying, and

(*188*)

Bob made the boys help him on one of the horses, and he, Bob, mounted the other. He then again offered the boys pay for the horses, but they refused to take it, when he ordered them to go straight home, and he and Jim got on the main road and proceeded to where they had promised to meet Cole, Bob telling Jim to keep in the lead and he would bring up the rear and protect him, and to make the best time he could, as it was necessary that they should get out of that country as quick as possible.

Another Fight with Their Pursuers.

After traveling about fifteen miles a party of armed men overtook them and at once commenced firing. A running fight continued for some time, Bob returning the fire, he having Jim's pistol as well as his own. Bob succeeded in killing one man and wounding another. During the fight Bob felt great anxiety for Jim's safety, and while leaning forward on his horse and urging Jim to retreat as fast as possible, a ball from one of the guns of the pursuing party struck him under the left shoulder blade, coming out on top of the shoulder. The pursuers at length gave up the chase and cared for their dead and wounded. About dusk that evening they arrived at the house of their friend, where they had promised to meet Cole, and they found him there, his wound having greatly improved. All three of the boys were now badly wounded, and they took to the brush, a short distance from the house, where a sort of hospital was erected, and Cole acted as surgeon, dressing the wounds and otherwise caring for the maimed. Cole being less disabled than either of the other boys, that night took both of the mares which had been pressed from the boys in the morning out on the road some fifteen miles and turned them loose, thinking they would return to their homes and colts. As was afterwards learned, they both went straight home.

Another Night Attack.

Horse stealing is a very common thing in that whole region of country, and the neighborhood in which the boys were now stopping had suffered in this line but a day or two previous and parties were then on the hunt for stolen horses and horse-thieves. The second night after their arriving at the house of their friend, who, by the way, had not long resided there, having moved from Missouri, a party on the hunt surrounded the house and used some harsh language towards the occupant, branding all Missourians as horse-thieves, and at length fired into the windows. The occupant of the house at once returned the fire, killing one, and then fled to where the boys were. It was afterwards learned that he had killed one of his nearest neighbors, but, though regretting it, felt conscious that the fault was clearly with the deceased.

Matters again assumed rather too lively an appearance for them, and the boys and their friend left for the residence of an acquaintance in the Choctaw Nation, after procuring horses, the Younger boys being in a very feeble condition. After reaching the Nation they traded a horse for a spring wagon, and then went to Western Texas, remaining there until their wounds were all healed up. They reached Western Texas in the month of July, 1874. Thus it will be seen that for about one month previous to their reaching Western Texas, it was one continued series of engagements with much superior numbers, and during this time a number of men were killed and many wounded, the Younger boys themselves receiving such wounds as but few men could bear up under, much less endure the hardships and privations which fell to their lot.

The Youngers Generally.

The Youngers went home after the surrender of the Southern Armies, and tried to live at peace with their old neighbors and friends. They were residents of Jackson county, Missouri, and for months it was a question whether this county would be held altogether by the Kansas people, or go back to Missouri. The county was in a state of anarchy. A vigilance committee went one night to the home of the Youngers, surrounded the house, attacked the female members, but found none of the men at home. Again and again this was done. Threats were made of certain death if any of them were caught, and word was sent them that they should not remain in the county. They were waylaid, and hunted down in every conceivable manner. They were compelled to protect themselves in the best possible manner, to go heavily armed, and thus were forced to assume the character of outlaws. Other and bad men took advantage of this condition of affairs to pillage and murder in their names. Every highway robbery in the West, especially if there was about it a deed of boldness and dash, was placed to their account, almost without knowing why, and suddenly these proscribed men were made both famous and infamous.

Propositions were made to both Governors McClurg and Woodson, only asking protection from mob-violence as the sole condition of a surrender. Neither of the Governors gave the required guarantee, and so nothing came of the efforts made, in good faith, to be once more at peace with society and the law. There was abundant reason why these men should not surrender unless the guarantee of protection was given, for men who had served in the same guerrilla band had been taken out at night from their places of imprisonment and hung by masked and unknown men. Tom Little was hung at Warrensburg, Johnson county; McGuire and Devon were hung at Richmond, Ray county; Arch. Clemens was shot in Lexington, Lafayette county; Al. Shepherd and Payne Jones were shot in Jackson county; in the same county Dick Burns was surprised, while asleep, and murdered. Many of Quantrell's men had to flee the country; many were hung and shot in other places. For months after hostilities had ceased, predatory and bloodthirsty bands, under the guise of vigilance committees, swept over the border counties, making quick work of Confederate guerrillas wherever they could be found.

For all crimes committed during the war the Congress of the United States had absolved the Federal soldiers. By a special law, Kansas granted absolution to all who had killed, robbed, burned or plundered, and held the militia free from any trial or prosecution for deeds done or crimes committed during the war. The present Constitution of Missouri provides that no person shall be prosecuted in any civil action or criminal proceeding for, or on account

(*194*)

of any act by him done, performed, or executed after January 1st, 1861, by virtue of military authority. Happening to be on the wrong side, however, these men are cut off from the benefits of all such amnesties or protective acts, and are outlaws simply because they were forced into an attitude of resistence in that transition period in Missouri when the very worst element of the population were gratifying their private feuds and vengeance. It has long since been an established fact that the Youngers cannot be taken alive by force, and all hopes of doing so by those who imagine they can capture them, to the mind of every man in the least acquainted with them, is perfectly ridiculous.

The Younger boys have a cattle ranch in Texas, which they call their home. When the semi-annual cattle "drive" comes up, however, it generally brings them back to their old haunts, and the homes of their friends in Missouri, in St. Clair, Jackson and other counties, where they remain a short time, visiting friends and relatives.

Years ago these boys were orphaned and driven out of Missouri, and the continued efforts of their enemies to persecute and hunt them down like wild beasts, has, very naturally, caused them to become reckless and at all times prepared for an emergency. They are men possessing but few of the lesser vices, and it is no uncommon thing to see them attending church, when they are in a neighborhood where there is no likelihood of trouble.

Almost every depredation committed in Missouri and the adjoining States, the past four or five years, has been laid to the Youngers or their friends. In fact, such has been their character, that it seemed an easy matter for others to commit depredations and escape detection. Within the past year, however, this has been discovered to be a great mistake, and since the few, if any, of the crimes committed, have been attributed to the Younger Brothers.

Miscellaneous Items.

The Hot Springs, Arkansas, stage robbery, which occurred in January, 1874, was one of the boldest robberies ever committed, eclipsing any of the feats attempted by the renowned Dick Turpin. Cole Younger was charged with having a hand in this little affair, but he is able to prove by some of the leading men of Carroll Parish, Louisiana, that he was there at the time. In his letter, published elsewhere, Cole Younger refers to this matter, and gives the names of gentlemen by whom he can prove his whereabouts at the time. This book being a pretty complete history of Western depredations during the past few years, we reprint the following account of this daring highway robbery, taken from the Little Rock, Arkansas, Gazette:

"From Mr. G. R. Crump, a representative of the wholesale tobacco and cigar house of Edmunds, Pettigrew & Co., of Memphis, who arrived from Hot Springs last night, and was on Thursday's stage, going to the Springs, at the time of the robbery referred to in Friday's Gazette, we learn the particulars of the affair. There was one stage and two light road wagons, or ambulances, the stage being in front and the other two vehicles immediately in the rear. At the Gains place, five miles this side of Hot Springs, the stage was stopped to water the stock. While watering, five men rode up, coming from toward Hot Springs, and passed on by. Each man wore a heavy blue army overcoat, but neither of them were masked. Nothing was thought of the matter, and the vehicles moved on. After going about half a mile, the men who had passed them at the Gains place, rode up from behind, and the first thing that Mr. Crump, who was in the first stage, heard, was an order to the driver to stop, or his head would be blown off. The stage was stopped, and, on throwing up the curtain, he saw a pistol pointed at him and the others in the stage, telling them to get out quick, accompanied by an oath. They got out, and as they did so, were ordered to throw up their hands. Three men were in front of them with cocked pistols and another with a shot-gun, while on the other side of the stage was still another, all pointing their weapons toward the passengers and the driver. After getting the passengers out they made them form in a kind of circle, so that all of them could be covered by the pistols and gun.

The leader then "went through" each passenger, taking all the watches, jewelry and money that could conveniently be found that were of special value. From ex-Gov. Burbank, of Dakota, they obtained $840 in money, a diamond pin and gold watch. A gentleman named Taylor, from Lowell, Mass., went up for $650 in money. A passenger from Syracuse, N. Y., gave up his last nickle, $160. Mr. Johnny Dietrich, our boot and shoe merchant, lost $5 in money and a fine gold watch. He had $50 besides this in the watch pocket of his pants which they did not find. Mr. Charley Moore, of the ice house, gave up $70 in money and his silver watch, but they returned the latter, stating they did not want any silver watches. A Mr. Peoples, who resides near Hot Springs, lost $20. Three countrymen lost about $15. The express package, containing about $450, was also taken. Mr. Crump had his watch and about $40 to $45 in money gobbled. After getting through with the passengers, they tore open several mail sacks in search of registered letters, but did not get any. While the main party was engaged in this work, another took out the best horse in the coach, saddled him, rode him up and down the road about fifty yards, two or three times, and remarked that "he would do."

(*198*)

After all this the captain went to each passenger in turn and questioned him as to where he was from, and inquired if there were any Southern men along. Mr. Crump spoke up, as did one or two others, that they were Southern men. They then asked if there were any who had served in the Confederate army during the war. Mr. Crump answered that he did. They questioned him as to what command, and remarking that he looked like an honest fellow, one who was telling the truth, handed him back his watch and money, saying they did not want to rob Confederate soldiers; that the Northern men had driven them into outlawry, and they intended to make them pay for it.

Coming to Mr. Taylor of Lowell, they asked where he was from.

"St. Louis," he responded.

The "captain" eyed him closely. "Yes, and you are a newspaper reporter for the St. Louis Democrat, the vilest paper in the West. Go to Hot Springs and send the Democrat a telegram about this affair, and give them my compliments."

Gov. Burbank asked them to return his papers, saying they could be of no benefit to them. The "captain" squatted down on his knees, and commenced examining then. Turning around to his followers he said, "Boys, I believe he is a detective—shoot him!" and forthwith he was covered with three pistols. "Stop," said the leader, looking further. "I guess it's all right," and handed the Governor his papers. Coming to the gentleman from Syracuse, New York, who was going to the Springs for his health, he asked them to give him back five dollars so that he could telegraph home. Eyeing him closely, the chief responded that if he had no friends or money, he had better go and die—that he would be little loss any way. The fellow with the shot-gun kept pointing it at the St. Louis Democrat man, as they termed him, making such cheerful remarks as these: "I'll bet I can shoot his hat off without touching a hair of his head."

All of them seemed to be jolly fellows, and enjoyed the fun very much. None of the passengers were armed, and, as Mr. Crump expressed it, "they had the drop on them." One passenger with the rheumatism, so badly afflicted that he could not get out of the coach, they did not touch, refusing to take anything he had.

A Skirmish at Neosho, Mo., with Illinois Troops.

After the battle of Elk Horn, Arkansas, all of the then enlisted Confederate troops were ordered East of the Mississippi river. This was in March, 1862. After the evacuation of the Trans-Mississippi department by the Confederate troops, this left all of the Confederate states then West of the river in danger of being overrun by the enemy. There were always a few men who kept in the rear of the main army, and when the Confederate troops crossed the river a few remained behind. Among those few who remained behind were some as brave men as ever handled a gun or carried a sword. They did not care to leave their homes and their wives, daughters, mothers and sisters unprotected.

Col. J. T. Coffee was one of the men who did not relish the idea of going East of the Mississippi river with the Confederate army, and remained West of the river. By the 15th of April he was busily engaged in Southwest Missouri

(*200*)

collecting together the deserters, or those who had neglected or refused to cross the river. Col. Coffee's headquarters were upon Cowskin Prairie, not far from Marysville, Arkansas, a small village upon the line or corner of Missouri, Arkansas and the Cherokee Nation, partly in Arkansas and partly in the Nation. It was a very suitable place to recruit a regiment of men, as the country was somewhat mountainous, interspersed with tracts of beautiful prairie land, which furnished excellent pasture for the animals. Fresh water springs also abounded, which furnished excellent water for both men and horses. It was not long until Col. Coffee had succeeded in recruiting or bringing together a batallion of 200 men. He was desirous of making up a regiment, in order to have sufficient force to release his daughter, Bettie, who had been seized and thrust into a Federal prison at Bolivar, Polk county, Missouri, simply because this young lady, very beautiful and accomplished, of eighteen summers, was a little talkative, and advocated the rights of the Southern people to defend their altars and their firesides, and the green graves of their sires, from the ruthlessness of the invader, the Northern soldiers, who were then reducing their once peaceful and happy country to a state of devastation, misery and want. In the estimation of the Federal authorities, Miss Bettie was calculated to "add fuel to the flames," and arouse the Southern heart to resistence. On this account she was arrested and placed in prison, where her influence could not be heard and felt.

But in this they were greatly mistaken, as her arrest and imprisonment soon became known, and the result was that it only had the effect of still more arousing every man who had the least spark of Southern feeling in his heart, or in whose veins coursed Southern blood.

Col. Coffee's battalion of 200 men were tolerably well armed with shotguns and squirrel rifles. With his battalion and the aid of Col. Stanwatie, who was a half-breed Cherokee Indian, commanding a regiment, then stationed in the Nation, about forty miles distant, Col. Coffee hoped to accomplish the great object of his desire, the release of his daughter. The Cherokees, it will be remembered, were deeply and zealously devoted to the cause of the South, and the regiment under the command of Col. Stanwatie was organized for the purpose of aiding the Southern cause. Col. Coffee made known his intentions to Col. "Watie," as he was often called, who willingly furnished 200 men, commanded by the Major of the regiment. Col. Watie was very anxious that Neosho should be taken, as he had attacked that place with about 150 men some time previous and failed, sustaining the loss of a few men and one piece of artillery, he having been overpowered in numbers and the enemy having the advantage of improved arms and war material. The brave commander had stood by his field-piece, firing as rapidly as possible, after his men had retreated in confusion, and did not leave until all chance of success had become utterly impossible.

With the addition of the battalion from Col. Watie's regiment, Col. Coffee thought his force sufficient to capture Neosho, which was sixty miles distant. After nightfall upon the 5th of May, Col. Coffee's men took up the line of march for Neosho, and by the next night were within two miles of the place. In approaching Neosho, the main road was not taken, but the most direct route, the untraveled paths, and at times no regard was had to roads, but the direct course, traveling, as it were, by the compass. The most of the country through which Col. Coffee passed was a barren waste, with flinty soil, and mountainous. The small flint mountains in this section of country are separated by deep gulches, in which the most luxuriant grass grows, which affords splendid grazing for stock. In one of these gulches, within two miles of the town of Neosho, Col. Coffee concluded to wait the approach of day on the morning of the 7th. Before the break of day on that morning Col. Coffee again took up the line of march, passing through the timber until within half a mile of the town. A halt was them made and most of the men dismounted, leaving but forty cavalrymen, commanded by Capt. Jackman. The Confederate forces advanced to the rear of a field, containing seven or eight acres, in a creek bottom, back of which field was heavy timber, with thick undergrowth, where the horses were left in charge of a small guard. By this time daylight had appeared. The infantry were then ordered into line, and marched through heavy black-oak timber just back of town. Capt. Jackman was ordered to take a plain road leading to town, on the left of the infantry. The road entered the town on the northwest, but Jackman was ordered to pass around town and enter from the southwest. The sun was now up, shedding its rays of light on all around, and the Federal camp was in full view. As they ascended a slight eminence, at the outward part of the town, they had a full view of the place, which is situated upon a piece of low land south of a small creek, the Federal camp being directly in front of the Confederate line of infantry. Capt. Jackman had fired upon

(*203*)

and captured the Federal outpost on the northwest. This occurred about the time Col. Coffee had got up within full view of the Federal camp, who were mostly up and engaged in getting breakfast. A charge was then ordered, which was made with a yell and determination that at once struck terror into the enemy's camp. As the charge was being made a frightened lady ran out of her house and got directly in front of the Confederate line, just as the Federals opened fire. Col. Coffee ordered two of his men to seize her and carry her into the house and close the door, which was done in a moment. Col. Coffee had given orders to his men to fire at the feet of the enemy, thereby insuring a more effective fire, if the orders were carried out, as it is a well known fact that all firing, in battle, ranges too high. Two rounds from the ranks of Coffee's men caused the enemy to break and retreat in confusion.

A second charge was ordered, which was successfully made and carried everything before it, and the Confederates were soon in the Federal camp, with the latter in full flight. Just then Capt. Jackman entered town upon the north. The enemy retreated towards Newtonia. As Jackman entered the town he discovered two Dutchmen, heavily armed, making across a field near by, and he ordered two of his men to throw down the fence, follow and capture them. As they neared them they were commanded to halt, when one of them turned around and fired, killing one of Jackman's men. This occurred within plain view of the command, and it filled the breast of every man with revenge, and, as if prompted by the same impulse, nearly the whole company rushed through the open gap to have revenge for the death of their comrade, which was speedily accomplished.

The enemy was pursued several miles by Capt. Jackman, and their wagons, camp equipage and some arms captured. Their flag was also captured and fell into the hands of the Cherokees, who made a constant display of it, in a very boastful manner. It seemed to be their hearts' joy to have the honor of capturing the enemy's flag. Thus a complete victory was achieved. The loss on both sides was very light.

The evening previous to the battle some of the Federals had boasted that they would have 'coffee for breakfast,' some having just arrived, but the Coffee they got was of a different character than they expected to relish, and their coffee served to complete the breakfast of Col. Coffee's men.

After the battle Col. Coffee fell back upon Grand River, in the edge of the Nation, where he remained camped for some days, until a Federal command from Kansas, composed of Kansas Jayhawkers and Pin Indians, 1,100 men, were in hot pursuit of him. The Cherokees had fallen back to Watie's Mill, and this left Coffee with less than 200 men, a force insufficient to compete with the Federals, and he also fell back to the same point.

The Battle of Poison Springs, Arkansas.

Warlike operations commenced in the Trans-Mississippi Department early in the spring of 1864. About the last of March the Federal authorities had devised or agreed upon a plan to carry on the war in the Western Department. Gen. Banks was to proceed up Red River to a certain point, disembark his troops, and march by land, passing through Louisiana and enter Texas upon the east, at a certain point. Gen. Steele was to move from Little Rock, Arkansas, with his troops, and those two armies were to unite or consolidate their forces in Texas and harvest the wheatfields of that State, carrying off all the cotton, &c. But Gen. Kirby Smith, who had command of all the Confederate forces of the Trans-Mississippi Department, was closely watching the Federal movements. About the last of March Major-General Sterling Price was ordered to Louisiana with all of his infantry, to oppose the movements of Gen. Banks. Gen. Price left all of his cavalry in Southern Arkansas, to confront the movement of Gen. Steele at Little Rock. Gen. Price and Gen. Dick Taylor, a son of old Zachariah Taylor, the hero of the battle of Buena Vista, Mexico, in 1848, combined their forces in Louisiana, at Mansfield. At this point a battle was fought, resulting in the routing of Gen. Banks with great loss. Gen. Steele began to move South about the same time, and was opposed by the cavalry of Gen. Marmaduke, Gen. Joe Shelby and Gen. Cabell, of Arkansas. All of the cavalry at this time was under the command, or subject to the orders of Gen. Marmaduke. He soon had heavy work to do, as Gen. Steele had a force of 16,000 men, while Gen. Marmaduke's whole command did not exceed 4,000 men. Heavy skirmishing soon commenced between the two commands, and was kept up every day from the first of April until the battle at Jenkin's Ferry, in which Gen. Steele was defeated by Gen. Price. All the Confederate cavalry could do was to keep the Federals in check until Gen. Price returned from Louisiana with his infantry. Gen. Marmaduke had heavy skirmishing with Steele's forces at

(*206*)

Spoonville and other places. He knew that Gen. Steele had four times his number and therefore avoided a general engagement.

As soon as Gen. Price and Gen. Taylor defeated Gen. Banks, Gen. Price returned to Arkansas with his infantry, coming upon Gen. Steele near Camden. Here Gen. Steele tried to induce Gen. Price to believe he intended making a stand, and as soon as he took possession of the town sent out a train of forage wagons, upon White Oak Creek, by the way of Poison Springs. With the train was a guard of 1,000 men. As soon as this information was obtained by Gen. Price, he sent out Gen. Greene of Missouri and Gen. Cabell of Arkansas, with their small brigades. They passed on up White Oak Creek some distance, until they came to where it forks. Gen. Green took his command up one fork and Gen. Cabell the other. After passing up these streams about four miles they came to a halt and waited for the enemy. During all this time Gen. Steele was moving his forces out of Camden, aiming to get to Little Rock. The forage wagons had been sent South. Thus it will be observed that his intention was to sell out that small force, well knowing they would be captured by the Confederate forces. The Federal forage train came down the north fork and opened fire on Gen. Cabell's troops, who returned the fire spiritedly. The train guard had two pieces of artillery. Gen. Cabell also had a battery of four guns, belonging to Col. Monroe's regiment. As soon as the enemy opened fire, Gen. Cabell sent a courier to Gen. Green, informing him that his troops were now engaged with the enemy, in a hot contest, and to move up his command at once. The courier returned with the information that he would soon be on hand with his command. By this time Gen. Cabell's troops were being driven back, with a heavy loss, when a second courier was sent to Gen. Green, telling him to hasten up on a double quick to his relief. The answer was soon received that Gen. Green was close at hand. Gen. Green had also sent back word to Gen. Cabell to get his men out of the way, as he, Green, intended to charge the enemy. Gen. Cabell did as directed. The enemy were now in an open field of about ten acres, when the Missourians came dashing in, in full charge, Gen. Green taking off his hat and holding it in his hand, leading the charge. Those noble and brave Missourians seemed to know no fear or danger, but rushed wildly into the field, scattering death and destruction all around. The Dutch and negroes of the Federal command fought well. It was a hand-to-hand contest, for half an hour. Some of the Dutch broke and ran from the field, but the most were killed in battle. The entire forage guard was composed of Dutch and negroes. Six hundred negroes were killed, as no quarters were given by the Rebels to them. Their guns, wagons, horses, &c., were all captured.

The Battle of Clear Creek, Mo.

This battle was fought on the second day of August, 1862, between some Missouri Confederate troops and Iowa Federals, being the First Iowa Cavalry, under the command of Col. Warren. The Missourians were from St. Clair county, and commanded by Capt. Handcock, who was afterwards promoted to the rank of Colonel. Some weeks previous to this small battle, so far as numbers on the Confederate side was concerned, although quite formidable on the part of the Federals, their loss being quite heavy, Capt. Handcock had been in St. Clair county, upon the banks of the Osage river, mustering together men, hoping to swell his number to a battalion, intending then to march them to the regular Confederate army, then in the State of Arkansas. At the time of the battle he had augmented his forces to near two hundred men, but only about seventy men were armed. Capt. Handcock's principal place of rendezvous was upon Clear creek. This creek is a small stream tributary to the Osage river, which takes its rise or heads near the northwest corner of Cedar county, and empties its waters into the Osage river three miles below Taborville, in St. Clair county. Upon the right bank of this stream, about six or seven miles from its mouth, in the timber, was Capt. Handcock and his men on the morning of the battle. At the time they were preparing to leave for the South, at the earliest possible moment, not anticipating an attack. Capt. Handcock had gathered together all the men he thought could be consolidated at the time. He felt confident that his whereabouts were known and thought it prudent to leave as soon as possible, as large Federal forces were within striking distance all around him. He did not suppose his exact position was known, but he felt assured that it was known he was in the county of St. Clair.

Some months before this Col. Warren had entered the county with one thousand cavalry. At this time he had his men divided up, a portion of them holding the post at Osceola, St. Clair county, a portion at Germantown, and a portion at Butler, both the latter places being in the adjoining county of Bates. As before stated, Capt. Handcock was getting ready to leave for the South, and would have been off in less than two hours after the fight commenced. A day or two previous he had also learned that Col. Coffee, Confederate, had captured the town of Greenfield, Dade county, Missouri, with most of the militia stationed there, and intended marching in that direction hoping to fall in with him.

Early upon the morning of the second of August, 1864, Capt. Handcock's pickets came into camp and reported that there was a body of men approaching from the west side of the timber. Five of Handcock's men, who were breakfasting at Mrs. McCulloch's a short distance from the camp, were captured. The Federal advance, which captured the five men at Mrs. McCulloch's, failed to get one man, and he watched an opportunity, and, with a revolver in each hand, made a dash on them and put them to flight to such an extent that his companions succeeded in making their escape.

As soon as Capt. Handcock learned of the approaching enemy, he formed his men in line of battle, selecting the best possible position for defence, which was a ravine along a field, the fence running along the field being very high, as the field or lot was used to keep mules secure. This ravine crossed the road near the field, and on both sides of the road the brush was quite thick, and down this road the Federals were expected to come. Capt. Handcock had all his horses taken back to a secure place and put in charge of a number of his men who were unarmed.

All of Handcock's men, with a very few exceptions, were raw recruits, who had never been under fire, and, as before stated, without arms, and unorganized. Most of the arms that were used were shotguns and squirrel rifles, with no prepared ammunition. Capt. Handcock had with him about one keg of powder, which, when divided up between his men, was a small allowance to each man, and required care and economy in its use. The ammunition was in charge of one man, and consequently on the morning of the fight, even up to the time of its actual commencement, the men were almost wholly without the means of resistance, and the distribution did not take place until after the men were placed in line of battle.

As soon as Capt. Handcock had made the preliminary arrangement of his men, he detailed a squad to go up the road towards the prairie, with instructions to decoy the Federals into the timber, opening fire on them as soon as they got within range, and if they hesitated to accept the challenge thus thrown out, to advance on them and force them into an engagement, and as soon as they found that the Federals were advancing to retreat on down the road, passing through their own ambushed lines, some forty or sixty yards, and then to wheel into the brush. Before the decoying squad started to lead the enemy into the trap prepared for them, one of the squad was detailed to keep in the rear on the retreat, thereby the more effectually inducing the Federals to follow, with the hope of at least capturing him.

Capt. Handcock arranged his men in a ravine, in line, ten feet apart, with instructions to fire directly to the front, but under no circumstances were they to fire until the head of the Federal cavalry reached a point directly opposite the head of their line, which would be known by the commencement of firing at the extreme head of the column.

When the Lieutenant, in command of the advance squad

or decoying party, reached the prairie, he discovered the foe not far distant, upon the open plain, and as they got sight of the rebel boys they began to place their men in readiness for battle. They seemed to be eager for rebel blood, and soon put the advance guard to flight, pursuing them hotly on clear through the rebel lines. Capt. Handcock heard the roaring of the feet of the approaching animals, as they came in hot pursuit of his companions, and again cautioned his men to hold their fire until all had passed the proper point. "Boys," said he, "do not become excited, but keep perfectly cool and reserve your fire until I give the signal with my pistol, and then take deliberate aim at the man directly in your front. By so doing your fire will be well directed, and each of you will get a man, and thereby do much greater execution than you could otherwise possibly do." A moment afterwards the enemy came in sight, and after the rebel squad had passed through and the Federal head got opposite Capt. Handcock, he let loose with his pistol and brought down his man, at the same time crying out, "Huzza, my brave boys," when about seventy guns sent forth their deadly missiles into the ranks of the enemy, and down went riders and horses, along the entire line. The foe at once checked up, and their men positively cried out for mercy so deadly and destructive was the fire of the rebel ranks. But as they did not offer to surrender, the rebels at once, as soon as they reloaded, gave them the second round. The Federals then crowded up along the fence which enclosed the mule lot, spoken of heretofore, and after partially recovering from the terrible shock, they returned the fire in the direction of the ravine. But the rebels soon gave them the third round, which caused them

(*212*)

to force their animals through and over the fence as best they could. A gap was made in the fence, and through this many a horse passed, though as he did so many a rider dropped dead. At length the Federals beat a hasty retreat.

Out of the two hundred Federals that came down the valley of Clear Creek, only about 120 escaped unhurt, nearly 80 falling dead in their tracks. The party was commanded by a Captain of Provost, Col. Warren not being with them. The entire Federal force sent out was 240 men, 40 being held back in reserve, but the reserve was never sent up. Capt. Handcock lost one man killed and two wounded. The man killed was Lee Bradley, of Bates county, Missouri, who left his position in the ravine and went out on the road, among the enemy, where he met his death. His grave now marks the battle-field. The Federal dead were hauled off to Butler, Bates county, after the fight.

As soon as the fight was over Capt. Handcock saw that his dead comrade was buried, the wounded cared for, and then took up his line of march for Dade county, Missouri. When the command arrived at the waters of Horse Creek, in Cedar county, a halt was ordered. While here the batallion was organized into companies and Capt. Handcock was elected Colonel. Here the guns of the men were arranged into squads according to their caliber, and ammunition prepared accordingly.

The line of march was again resumed and the command finally arrived at the headquarters of Col. J. T. Coffee, in Dade county, Mo., where the men were transferred to the regular Confederate army.

Fight at Port Union, Kansas.

During the fall of 1864, at the time of Gen. Price's last raid into Missouri, after the battle of Big Blue, Gen. Price entered Kansas and passed on South through the eastern portion. After passing by Fort Scott, a Lieutenant commanding 85 men, struck out across the country for Fort Union, Kansas, a small inland town containing a few dry goods stores, &c. Our informant says he never saw so much canned fruit in so small a place as this in his life. The place was garrisoned by 125 Federal troops. As Gen. Price's army had passed on South, this inland post had no fears from that source, as it was thought. The Commander of those 85 Confederates was a man who loved to fight whenever an opportunity offered itself, and there was anything like an equal chance to gain a victory. His men were all equally willing, and in fact had frequently been termed "blood-hounds," so eager were they to engage in battle. When the Confederates got within about one mile of the Fort they met a man who had just left there, and who was questioned about the number of troops there and all the particulars possible to obtain from him. He stated that there were about 25 men in the Fort, and the remainder, about 100, had left their guns inside the Fort and were scattered over the place drunk, as they had learned that Gen. Price had gone on South, hotly pressed by the Federal forces, and they concluded to have a jolly drunk in order to commemorate the event.

After parting with the man from the Fort the company started off in a gallop and did not slacken their speed until they entered the town, and then dashed into the

(*214*)

Fort, completely taking the Federals by surprise, who were not aware of their presence until they commenced dealing out death and destruction on every side. The few inside the stockade were soon shot down and none left to tell the tale. After the terrible slaughter in the Fort, which was but the work of a few moments, the Confederates left the garrison and proceeded to town, which was situated in the prairie, near a clump of timber, where many of the Federal soldiers took refuge as soon as they heard the firing at the fortifications, but a short distance off. Some had mounted their horses and rode off across the prairie, in the direction of a creek, about two miles distant, but they were hotly pursued and shot down, not being able to make much resistance, having left their guns inside the Fort, though most of them had side-arms, which they used to the best possible advantage, and in several instances a hand-to-hand fight took place. But few escaped, nearly the whole of the Federal force was left dead upon the field of battle, as food for the cayotes that so numerously abound in that section. Those who took refuge in the timber were charged upon by a portion of the Rebel cavalry, and most of them likewise fell victims of Rebel bullets.

After the fight was over it is said one could have walked some distance up the main street on dead men and horses, along the saloons. The whole time consumed in the fight was not over one hour, but it was a terrible slaughter, as nearly the whole Federal garrison were left dead upon the field of battle. The Rebel loss was one man killed and one wounded, the wounded man recovering in a short time. After the battle the Rebels entered the stores and helped themselves to such eatables as they could find, not in the last

(*215*)

slighting the canned fruit, which was so plentiful, and quite a luxury to hungry and fatigued soldiers. After they had all helped themselves to something to eat, they then proceeded to dress themselves up in the best suits of clothing in the stores, which were in great abundance. They then mounted their horses and left the bloody and sacked town to its fate, striking across the prairie in a southerly direction, and entered the camp of their leader, Gen. Price, the next day, about night-fall.

LETTER FROM AN OLD CITIZEN OF MISSOURI.

Col. Harry W. Younger was murdered by a party of Union Soldiers, so called, and backed by the Government of the United States, but in truth and reality nothing more nor less than an organized band of thieves and cut-throats, who were a disgrace to any government. This brutal and highway murder and robbery took place on the western border of Missouri. This same party were of the number who drove Coleman and James Younger, sons of Col. Harry W. Younger, into the camp of Quantrell. These boys, left to themselves and not harrassed by the militia, were not disposed to hurt any one, and if they could have had their choice, would have remained quietly at home during the whole war, and attended to the farms of their father. But how could it be possible for them to do so, and time after time to see and hear the many depredations and outrages that were being committed upon their parents? Their father robbed of his property, then waylaid, murdered and robbed of the money he had just received for a lot of stock which he had sold; their old mother insulted and abused, compelled to fire her own house with her own hands, driven from place to place, harrassed and deviled to such an extent that she at length filled an early grave. All these things are true to the very letter and well known to hundreds of as good citizens as ever lived in Missouri. These things, and many others of less importance, all tended to drive the Younger boys to desperation and to induce them to seek revenge upon those who had perpetrated the outrages. It was but natural for them so to do. They would not have been human to do otherwise. That Cole Younger did seek out and shoot down some, perhaps nearly all, of the men who murdered his father, there seems to be little doubt. It is also true that there still lives one of the prime movers and plotters of the murder of his father, and who to this day carries the valuable gold watch taken from the body of Col. Younger after he had been murdered; and it is also true that Cole Younger did prevent John Younger from taking the life of this same guilty and heartless wretch about two years ago at Monegaw Springs, in St. Clair county. The party of murderers and robbers consisted of ten men, and those more intimate with them and the whole circumstance than the writer of this, have assured me that nine met their just deserts and filled untimely graves, leaving, as before stated, yet one of the most guilty, unharmed, whose life seems to be a miserable one indeed, as it is said that he is scarcely ever seen outside of his house. Col. H. W. Younger, as was well known, was a staunch Union man at the breaking out of the war, and, therefore, there could be no excuse for the treatment he received at the hands of those calling themselves Union men; they were not Union men, they were Union thieves. What must be the remorse of conscience of the poor, miserable creature who still lives, when he reflects on his past life and conduct? Methinks I can see that man at the dark and dreary hour of midnight, when all is silent and still as the grave, tossing to and fro upon his couch, unable to sleep, with a vision of his murdered victim standing before him; with his life-blood oozing from the wounds of his mangled body. A resident of the town in which this man now lives, asserts that he is scarcely ever seen on the streets in daylight, but stealthily sneaks out at night, in disguise. Those who claim to be cognizant of the fact, also assert that there are now living near the town of Butler two widows, whose husbands were shot down in cold blood by the orders of this same individual, who was then acting as Captain. Notwithstanding this, this miserable creature is allowed to live in that community unpunished and unharmed, save that punishment inflicted upon him by an Allwise Providence.

Before the war it is said this same man was miserably poor, but now he seems to have plenty of this world's goods and lives in good style. He owns two farms, runs a livery stable and store, but where or when he got the money, no one knows but himself.

With regard to how the Younger boys make a living, if they do not commit robberies, a question very often asked but seldom answered correctly, I will give some facts well known to me. Nearly ever since the war these boys have had a cattle ranch in Western Texas, where they herd a large number of cattle, which are usually sold every fall and shipped north and east. Those acquainted with this business well understand the large profits arising therefrom, and can easily account for the fact that at times these boys have plenty of money, particularly when they visit Missouri, which is usually in the fall. During the summer of 1873, these boys visited Monegaw Springs, in St. Clair county, Missouri, where there were hundreds of persons stopping at the time, partaking of the curative waters. At these Springs their grandfather, Chas. F. Younger, spent the latter years of his life. He died in 1873, within five miles of the Springs, surrounded by many old acquaintances and friends, some of whom ranked among the oldest citizens of St. Clair county. Whenever the Younger Brothers passed through this portion of the State they always stopped to see their grandfather as well as visit other acquaintances. On this account some of the old citizens of St. Clair county, who are "well to do" farmers, have been accused of harboring and protecting horse-thieves, murderers, &c. Suffice it to say that those few old citizens whom the Youngers do visit when in this section of the state, cannot believe that the Youngers are guilty of what they have been so frequently charged, while in several instances they know from their own personal knowledge that the charges are false, as the boys were at their houses the very times they are charged with being hundreds of miles away committing depredations. Stealing and depredations of every kind have been the order of the day ever since the close of the war, and instead of diminishing, they seem to increase year after year, and in almost every instance, unless the parties are at the time apprehended, some newspapers take up the old cry of Younger Brothers, and soon it is heralded forth all over the country. Occasionally some newspaper editor or correspondent ventures to assert that the Youngers had nothing to do with the affair, but so general seems to be the belief that the Youngers are the only ones who can perpetrate such acts of lawlessness, that their assertions are drowned in the great cry of "Younger Brothers." This very forcibly reminds me of the story told of an old Quaker, in Philadelphia, many years ago. A dog went into his kitchen and stole a leg of mutton, and on learning the fact the old Quaker took after him, up the street, crying out in a loud voice, "bad dog, bad dog." The cry of "mad dog" was immediately taken up by those passing, when every one took after him and very soon succeeded in killing him. When the Quaker arrived and found that the crowd had killed him, he asked why they had done so. Why, said one, did you not cry out "mad dog?" no, replied the Quaker, I said "bad dog," for so he is; he stole my meat. So it is with the Younger Brothers; they have been bad during the war, and did, possibly, revenge the murder of their father and cruel treatment of their mother, but further than this, since the war terminated, nothing wrong can be proven against them.

For some time after the occurrence Cole Younger was accused of having a hand in the Iowa train robbery, which occurred on Monday morning, July 21st, 1873, while it can be proven by 20 or 30 of the most respectable men in St Clair county, Missouri, that he was at Monegaw Springs on Sunday afternoon, the 20th of July, not over 15 hours before the robbery took place, and could not possibly have been there. Did he possess the wings of the fleetest bird of the air, he could not have passed from Monegaw Springs to Iowa, to the place where the robbery occurred.

I am in no way connected with the Youngers, by family ties or blood relation, neither have I any sympathy with men who I believe do wrong, but I think that justice should be done to all, and therefore have penned this letter for your work about to be published, which, should you think proper, you are at liberty to use.

Respectfully Yours, &c.,

S. M. O.

To A. C. Appler.

The Nevada Stage Robbery.

About the 10th or 12th of August, 1873, four brigands stopped a stage in Nevada Territory, which carried Wells, Fargo & Co.'s safe, and robbed it of a large sum of money. Mr. E. Baldwin, Chief Engineer of the Davenport (Iowa) & St. Paul Railroad, who was a passenger on the stage, gives the following account of the robbery:

Four men sprang from behind rocks, seized the leaders by the bit, and bade the driver "get down from there." It was some time before the passengers could understand the interruption, but at last they were made to comprehend it without much ceremony. The driver was ordered to take the horses from the coach and lead them to one side. He obeyed. Next the passengers were told to "dismount" and seat themselves on a redwood log. As each of the robbers held a double-barreled shot-gun, and swore that somebody's brains would be spilled unless "you step right lively now," the order was obeyed with alacrity. The passengers sat still as mice under the cover of the shot-guns, and silently watched the operations of the robbers in getting at the contents of the safe. The scoundrels drilled holes about the lock, and elsewhere in the door, poured powder in the openings, tamped them, and then lighted the fuse. In a half minute there was a thick puff of smoke, a dull heavy sound, and there lay the safe open. It was but the work of a minute to sack the bags of gold and packages of greenbacks, and then the robbers ordered the passengers to "mount." The travelers obeyed, and took their seats; then the driver was ordered to "hitch up," and he did as he was told—and was requested to "drive on quick, and not lag once for a mile." And the four-horse team flew away from the locality in locomotive speed. The robbers gobbled between $8,000 and $12,000.

The Quincy, Illinois, Bank Robbery.

The night of the 12th and 13th of February, 1874, the First National Bank of Quincy, Illinois, was robbed of nearly a half million dollars. On the morning of the 13th, the porter, on going into the bank, discovered that the ceiling and walls near the vault were badly shattered. He at once notified the officials, when an investigation was made. It was soon discovered that the vault door could not be unlocked. An exploration was made in the second story of the building where an opening was found in the hall floor through which the burglars had descended on the top of the vault. Further examination showed that a hole over three feet square had been drilled through three feet of solid masonry, and a plate of boiler iron two feet square cut from the lining of the vault with chilled chisels. This done access was obtained to the interior of the vault, where were two safes, one containing the money and special deposits of the bank, and the other government bonds and valuable papers. The money safe was found with the doors blown off their hinges and depleted of all its contents, save a bag of gold. There was in it $90,000 in currency belonging to the bank, $200,000 in Adams county bonds worth par, and special deposits of greenbacks and government bonds that run the total up to $500,000. The other safe containing valuable papers and bonds was also charged with powder and blasted, but did not yield, and its contents were safe.

The manner of working, after reaching the interior of the vault, was as follows: Powder was drilled into the cracks around and between the hinges of each safe, and

(*221*)

held fast by the free use of putty. A connection fuse was then adjusted to set both blasts off at once, and then passed through a rubber hose to the top of the highest safe, where a small pistol was screwed on an old ledger and so arranged that when it was discharged it set off the fuse. The pistol was fired by means of a cord which led from the vault to the street, and thus the burglars set off the explosion when the vicinity of the bank was clear of people. Several persons in adjacent buildings heard the sound and felt the concussion, but thought it nothing serious.

We believe it was not charged that any of the Youngers had a hand in this.

The Martling, Missouri, Safe Robbery.

On the 29th of August, 1873, the safe of Messrs. Crowder, Winn & Co., Commission Merchants of Martling, Southwest Missouri, and Agents of the Adams' Express Company, was blown open and robbed of about $4,000 in cash and some silver ware.

The Osceola, Missouri, Savings Bank.

On the morning of the 14th of March, 1875, about two o'clock, an attempt was made to rob the Osceola Savings Bank, at Osceola, St. Clair county, Missouri, by three young men living in the vicinity of town, named James Henley, William Henley and John Longdon. They had also taken into their confidence a young man living in town named William Hurt, but he repented before the feat was attempted to be accomplished, and conveyed the information to Mr. William O. Mead, the Cashier of the bank. Mr. Mead made the necessary preparations to receive the thieves, by engaging the services of some half dozen men and having them secreted and armed for the occasion. The boys were allowed to bore off the lock of the back door, when they were fired upon by several men stationed in Masonic Hall, which building adjoins the bank building, extending some twenty feet further back, to the alley. One of the men, John Longdon, was wounded, and captured shortly afterwards, and one other, William Henley, was arrested near Fort Scott, Kansas, about ten days afterwards. An ox team had been procured and hitched up, with which they expected to carry off the bank safe, it not being a very large one, yet much too large for those boys to have handled. The safe was in the back part of the bank building, near the door. The door is about four feet from the ground, and it was their intention to back the wagon up to the door and roll the safe on it. The wagon to be used was a heavy one, belonging to the sawmill of Alton, Sutherland & Co., and had been prepared for the occasion that night, by placing heavy oak planks on it. The whole thing was admirably planned, and worthy of older heads and hands at such business. It was their intention to convey the safe some distance down the river, in the hills, where they intended to break it open and secure the money it contained, about $12,000. Had it not been for young Hurt, who divulged the plan, and had they fully succeeded in their designs without being discovered, it is certain that the Youngers would have been credited with this robbery.

Store Robbed Near Clinton, Mo.

A most daring robbery occurred at the store Mr. D. C. Lambert, twelve miles north of Clinton, Henry county,

Missouri, about six o'clock on the evening of the 13th of May, 1875. The location of this robbery, as the reader will perceive, is not over forty miles from Monegaw Springs, St. Clair county, the neighborhood where the Youngers stay when in this section of Missouri. Two men entered the store and called for cigars, and while Mr. Lambert's back was towards them, they drew their revolvers, thrust them in his face, and commanded him to "hold up his hands." Two more men then entered, drew their revolvers and demanded money. Mr. Lambert then gave them all he had, about $150, when the leader of the party demanded of Lambert that he disclose the whereabouts of some $3,000 or $4,000 in gold, which his neighbors said he had secreted somewhere, on failure of which he was to suffer death. A young lady happened to come into the store about this time, and seeing the situation of affairs, threw herself between the robbers and Mr. Lambert, and begged of them to spare his life. The outlaws then discussed the propriety of hanging Lambert, but if they really had any intention of so doing did not carry it into execution. About this time another of the robbers, who had remained outside, politely asked two ladies and two gentlemen, who were playing croquet in the rear of the store building, to step inside, which they did without many unnecessary words, on discovering that the fellow was armed. The whole party were then placed under guard and told to keep quiet, but one of the scoundrels remained on watch in the store, while each door of the building was guarded by another of them. The leader then made a thorough search of the building, examining all trunks, boxes, &c., but found no traces of the $3,000 or $4,000 he spoke

(*224*)

of. He found, however, three revolvers, one gun and $11 of money belonging to the Shawnee postoffice, all of which was carried off. The party also helped themselves to such goods as they wanted. The loss of Mr. Lambert, in all amounted to about $300. They remained about one hour and a half, keeping their prisoners under guard all the while, until they were all mounted, when they rode rapidly off. Everything was conducted so calmly and quietly, that a blacksmith fifty yards distant knew nothing of the affair until the robbers left. They were all young men, well armed, and mounted on splendid animals. This robbery, like almost every other one of a similar character, where great boldness and skill are shown, has been charged to the account of the Younger Brothers, although neither of the boys had been seen in the State for six months previous. No clue to the robbers has ever been obtained.

Proposed Pardon of the Youngers and James Boys.

Gen. Jones, an eminet lawyer of Calloway county, and member of the Missouri House of Representatives, introduced the following into that body about the first of March, 1875, which, however, owing probably to the late time at which it was presented, failed to pass the Legislature. It received the approval of the Attorney-General, as well as many able lawyers of the State of Missouri. The following is the full bill:

Whereas, Equality is the essence of true Democracy, and no distinctions in person or class should ever be made by law, under a government of the people possessed of virtue, intelligence and true courage; and

Whereas, By the 4th section of the 11th article of the Constitu-

(*225*)

tion of Missouri all persons in the military service of the United States, or who acted under the authority thereof in this State, are relieved from all civil liability and all criminal punishment for all acts done by them since the 1st day of January, A. D. 1861; and

Whereas, By the 12th section of the said 11th article of said Constitution, provision is made by which under certain circumstances may be seized, transported to, indicted, tried and punished in distant countries, any Confederate or other person under band of despotic pleasure, thereby contravening the Constitution of the United States and every principle of enlightened humanity; and

Whereas, Such discrimination evinces a want of manly generosity and statesmanship on the part of the party imposing, and of courage and manhood on the part of the party tamely submitting thereto.

Whereas, Under the outlawry pronounced against Jesse W. James, Frank James, Coleman Younger, Robert Younger and others, who gallantly periled their lives and their all in the defence of their principles, they are of necessity made desperate, driven as they are from the fields of honest industry, from their friends, their families, their homes and their country, they can know no law but the law of self-preservation, can have no respect for and feel no allegiance to a government which forces them to the very acts it professes to deprecate, and then offer a bounty for their apprehension, and arms foreign mercenaries with power to capture and kill them; and

Whereas, Believing these men too brave to be mean, too generous to be revengeful, and too gallant and honorable to betray a friend or break a promise; and believing further that most, if not all the offences with which they are charged have been committed by others, and perhaps by those pretending to hunt them, or by their confederates; that their names are and have been used to divert suspicion from and thereby relieve the actual perpetrators; that the return of these men to their homes and friends would have the effect of greatly lessening crime in our State by turning public attention to the real criminals, and that common justice, sound policy and true statesmanship alike demand that amnesty should be extended to all alike of both parties for all acts done or charged to have been done during the war; therefore, be it

Resolved by the House of Representatives, the Senate concurring therein:

That the Governor of the State be and he is hereby requested to issue his proclamation notifying the said Jesse W. James, Frank James, Coleman Younger, Robert Younger and James Younger, and others, that full and complete amnesty and pardon will be granted them for all acts charged or committed by them during the late civil war, and inviting them peaceably to return to their respective homes in this State and there quietly to remain, submitting themselves to such proceedings as may be instituted against them by the courts for all offences charged to have been committed since said war, promising and guaranteeing to them and each of them full protection and a fair trial therein, and that full protection shall be given them from the time of their entrance into the State and his notice thereof under said proclamation and invitation.

The James and Youngers.

A Plea for Mercy from a Union Soldier and a Republican.

ST. LOUIS, March 15, 1875.

TO THE EDITOR OF THE GLOBE:

In your issue of last Saturday, the 13th, I read with much interest a communication against the granting of any amnesty to the James and Youngers. It was postmarked Charleston, Mo., and signed "Confederate." For the same reasons that "Confederate" selected the *Globe* as his "medium for reaching the public ear," so do I, a Republican, a Federal soldier, who belonged to the Second Colorado Cavalry, who fought the James and Youngers on twenty different occasions, who knows something of their history, and who believes as firmly as he believes in truth and justice that they have been lied upon by public opinion, slandered, and put in the attitude of the traditional dog who has to be hung because he has an ill name.

I do not propose to speak for the *Dispatch,* or defend the *Dispatch*—for the *Dispatch* is perfectly competent to do that for itself—but I do ask the *Globe* to give both sides of this subject, as I know the *Globe* is always willing to do for every question. As it happens, I claim to know as much about these famous men as "Confederate," although my opportunities for information were not as favorable as his, probably, because of the color of the uniform that clothed each of us; but one thing I am absolute in my belief of, and that is it is time for the war to be over in truth. Many things were done on the border by both sides that should have been forgotten when peace came, and when an impartial history comes to be written, it will be found that among the Guerrillas who wore the blue, and the Guerrillas who wore the gray, there was not even the difference of a single desperate deed the less on either side.

To answer "Confederate" as I think he should be answered, it will be necessary for me to ask sufficient space at your hands to take up his charges seriatim, and dispose of them by such references to establish facts as may be verified by any impartial man who chooses to make an investigation of them. His first reference is to the robbery of the Gallatin Bank, in Davies county, Missouri; the killing of its cashier, Captain John W. Sheets, and the subsequent pursuit of the robbers into Clay county. I was in Kansas City at the time this took place. Indeed, from the mustering out of our regiment until 1873, I lived in various portions of Jackson county, and among the worst and most desperate of the survivors of the bands of Quantrell, Todd and Anderson—men whom I had fought daily, sometimes getting the best and sometimes the worst of the fighting—and I never saw a more peaceful and law-abiding set of people, and never people more willing to let by-gones be by-gones. I know that the Jameses were accused of this attack on the bank, but I know further, that they published in the Kansas City *Times* nearly a column of affidavits from some of the best known and most respectable citizens of Clay county, attesting their innocence of this charge. One of these affidavits was signed by a well known Justice of the Peace, and another by the present Sheriff of the county, Captain John C. Groom. I give his name so that he may be referred to if anybody so desires. The affidavits are positive in the declaration that Jesse and Frank James were seen and talked to only a few hours before and after the robbery was perpetrated, and that it was a physical impossibility for them to have been in Kearney one hour, and eighty odd miles off in Gallatin the next, and back again eighty odd miles in Kearney the third hour. These affidavits are on file, and were sworn to and executed by as truthful men as there are in Missouri.

The next charge is made against the Youngers, and a reference is made to the fight in St. Clair county, in which John Younger had been killed. Now, John Younger had never been even accused of having a hand in any robbery. No reward was out for him. Coleman and James Younger had, but one hundred good citizens of St. Clair county would have come forward at any time to John Younger's constant presence at home. He was the mainstay of a family of helpless girls. The father had been killed at the begin-

ning of the war by Kansas men. The mother had been forced, with
a pistol at her head, to set fire to her own house, and to go on foot
for shelter through a deep snow to a neighbor's. From this exposure, a disease was contracted which soon put her in her grave.
Acting under the belief that the Youngers had been engaged in
the robbery of the Iron Mountain Railroad, at Gad's Hill, a posse
of detectives went into St. Clair county in search of them. The
hunted men—having the same love of life that is implanted in the
breast of everybody—turned out to hunt their pursuers. It was the
intention of the Youngers to disarm the detectives, and for this
purpose called upon them to surrender, having first "got the drop"
on them. It was done, apparently, the detectives threw down their
arms; but from all the evidence now before me, I am certain that
Lull was so excited when he shot John Younger that he did not
know what he was doing. He had but a single-barrel pistol; he
could only hope, at the best, to kill one of the brothers, while the
other brother, unharmed and heavily armed, would be absolutely
certain to have revenge. Lull had been the first man to call upon
his comrades to throw down their arms, and had himself cast off
a brace of navy revolvers, still retaining a derringer, however,
which he used when John Younger, supposing the whole party
without weapons, had quite carelessly uncovered them with his
double-barreled shot-gun. If Lull had meant to fight, he should
have fought just as soon as the Younger party came in sight; but
instead of doing this he called for a surrender, and set the example
himself of throwing his pistols on the ground, and then treach-
erously shooting one of the Youngers after he had been the means
of putting the lives of his own comrades in desperate jeopardy. It
was not war, common sense, fair dealing as between friends, nor
the act of a brave man. James Younger, when he saw his brother
John shot down, had but one thing to do—kill. And he did. He
was not the assailant in the light that "Confederate" puts it. He was
merely endeavoring to disarm men and keep them from killing
him who had openly boasted of their intentions, and who were
working for blood money, merely because it was the suspicion at
Pinkerton's headquarters that the Youngers had robbed the Gad's
Hill railroad train.

And now, Mr. Editor, a word or two in relation to this Gad's Hill robbery. Sometime last fall Governor Woodson wrote to Mr. Thomas Allen, as I have been reliably and semi-officially informed, and stated to him that he knew the whereabouts of the Youngers, and that if he, Allen, would furnish the necessary affidavit to the effect that they had robbed his train, or that he believed they had, he would have them arrested at once. Mr. Allen replied that he had employed able detectives himself, that Pinkerton's detectives had also been at work on the case, that a thorough examination of all the circumstances attending the outrage had been made, and that, so far from making an affidavit that the Youngers were at Gad's Hill, he could much more conscientiously make an affidavit that they had not been there. And yet for this robbery "Confederate" denounces them without knowing a single fact of the case, except what was published in the flaming sensation reports of the newspapers, and yet for this robbery they and the James brothers are made notorious from one extent of the land to the other.

I never met either of these men except on the battle field. They were with Jo. Shelby in 1874, with his notorious advance, led by Arthur McCoy and the quiet and desperate Jim Wood, now Circuit Clerk of Pettis county, and I was in Captain Kingsbury's company, of the Second Colorado. We held the rear of Curtis' retreating division, which, under Jim Lane, had been driven with some confusion from Lexington by General Shelby. Our regiment and this advance of Shelby's met hand-to-hand this side of Independence, about four miles. It was a desperate fight. Nothing could stop Shelby's charge. We killed George Todd there, one of the worst guerrillas the world every produced. Shelby's men killed our Major, Smith, a noble and brave soldier. We kept falling back and fighting, and they kept crowding us and fighting until darkness stopped the slaughter. I understand that on the staff of the *Dispatch*—the paper which "Confederate" condemns rather strongly for its advocacy of amnesty—is one of Shelby's soldiers. If that be so, he will bear me out in the assertion that never brave men met braver men than when the Second Colorado and Shelby's leading regiment came together at intervals for one long autumn day in 1864. And now I, as a Federal soldier, join with the *Dispatch* in asking amnesty for these men. It is the best thing that can be done. Kansas passed an oblivion act for all her soldiers, and I tell you Lane, Jennison, Montgomery, Goss and Cleveland did things in Missouri and Arkansas that could never have been surpassed by things done by Anderson, Quantrell, Todd, Poole, Thrailkill, the Jameses or the Youngers.

I know that when the war was over, the Youngers came home and tried to live like the balance of the guerrillas on both sides. Vigilant Committees drove them away. Many of their old comrades were waylaid, shot, and assassinated. Some who surrendered to take a trial for charges preferred against them, were hung at night by armed and masked men. It was the same case with the Jameses. They were waylaid; one of them was badly wounded from the brush, their mother's life and the lives of their families were placed in peril, and, of course, these men had to do the next best thing, they had to put on arms and defend themselves. Every robbery committed in the West for the past eight years has been put upon them. And, as an illustration of the unfairness and in justice of the newspapers—the only real manufacturers, after all, of public opinion—it will be only necessary to recall the fact that, on the day the train was robbed at Muncie, Kansas, a bank was also robbed at Corinth, Miss., and one in Tennessee. In each case the telegraph reported the Jameses and Youngers present, and, from that day to this, a contradiction of the hurtful lie has never been made nor never will.

I claim that these men should have a chance, and I have a right to urge this, knowing that men with war records just as bad, on our side, have received rewards and promotions. It cannot be denied truthfully by anybody that they tried to live in peace after the war closed, and that they were not permitted to do so. As soon as they were forced into the brush by proscription, everything mean and outrageous was laid at their door. The State can afford to give them a chance now, and thus break up a whole band of thieves and robbers who are committing depredations in their names.

REPUBLICAN.

The Bank Robbery.

About 2 o'clock on the afternoon of September 7th, 1876, eight men entered the town of Northfield, Minnesota, and proceeded to the bank. Three entered it and sprang over the counter, and ordered the cashier, J. L. Haywood, with a knife at his throat, to open the vault. At the same time, all persons in the bank, A. E. Bunker, cashier, his assistant and Frank Wilcox, clerk, were ordered to hold up their hands. Mr. Haywood refused to obey orders and open the money vault. His neck had been slightly scratched with a knife. Still persisting, the robbers put the muzzle of a pistol to his right temple and fired. Haywood fell dead. They then turned to Mr. Bunker and ordered him to open the vault. He said he did not know the combination. As the robbers made demonstrations towards him he ran out the back door. They fired at him, shooting him through the shoulder. Mr. Wilcox was not interfered with. While this was transpiring within, people of the city without were doing good work. Two of the robbers were killed outright and one wounded. The wounded man was taken away by his confederates. One of their horses was killed and one captured. The robbers did not get into the vault, nor did they find the cashier's drawer except the nickel drawer, and a handful of nickels taken from it was thrown to the floor. Four of the eight came to town before midday, and waited on the north side of the bridge till the other four came into town from Dundas. The men were all well mounted and armed with navy revolvers, with cartridges, in belts around their bodies. When the robbers crossed the bridge entering town they drew revolvers, and putting their horses into full gallop dashed through the street, shouting to the people on the walks to get inside. While the three men were engaged in the bank the others stood on the street threatening to shoot any one who interfered, and firing several harmless shots. Pistols and guns were quickly secured by citizens, and a young man named Wheeler from the window of the opposite building picked off one of the villains, shooting him through the heart. Another shot thought to be from Wheeler immediately after prostrated another, when the robbers mounted their horses and beat a retreat. A third robber was hit but escaped. A band of fifty citizens was organized, and headed by Wheeler started in pursuit.

On the 8th fourteen of the citizens in pursuit of the robbers overtook them late in the afternoon in a ravine a short distance from Shieldsville, when a number of shots were exchanged, killing one of the horses of the pursued. In all about 400 men were pursuing them. Gov. Pillsburg offered a reward of $1,000 for each of the robbers. Intense excitement prevails throughout that whole section of country.

A dispatch of the 10th states that the citizens are in hot pursuit, with a prospect of capturing or killing the band.

On the 12th the horses and saddles of the robbers were found in the timber near Cleveland.

The pursuit was continued from day to day until the afternoon of the 21st, when word was received from Sheriff McDonald, of Sioux City, that he had killed one of the robbers and captured three others, two of whom were mortally wounded; his party consisting of about 150 men. They were captured near Madelia, Watonwan county, Minnesota. They were pursued to a swamp, which was completely surrounded and the men gradually closed in upon them, keeping up a continuous fire, which was returned by the four robbers until one of their number was killed and two others supposed to be mortally wounded, and then only did they surrender. After being taken prisoners, two of them confessed to the Sheriff that they were the Younger Brothers, but refused to tell who their dead comrade was.

In the afternoon of the 22d, one of the editors of the *St. Paul Pioneer Press* went to Madelia and interviewed the Bandits. He says:

"I first called on Cole and James Younger, who occupy a bed together. Both are terribly wounded, and their faces much disfigured. They certainly do not look like such desperadoes as they are. Cole, who has bright red whiskers, had his right eye bandaged, and said he was suffering from seven wounds. James has a fearful looking mouth, the lower jaw bone being shattered. I told them I represented the *Pioneer Press*, and asked if they wished to say anything to the public. Cole was much obliged, and asked if I would kindly express their thanks to the citizens of Madelia, who had treated them with wonderful kindness. He expressed his surprise at such treatment, and was grateful for it. The doctor would not allow them to talk much, and as curious people were passing in and out, I left them to call on Bob.

These men suffer much, and their talk is sometimes deliri-
ous. Both are brave, never moaning, and are receiving every
possible attention. I found Bob, as he asked to be called
for short, lying in bed, shackled and suffering from a
wound in the arm received at Northfield, and from a wound
in the breast got yesterday. He was pleasant, cheerful and
communicative. He is a six-foot boy, 23 years old, and
as fine looking a specimen of manhood as I ever saw. He
has a kind expression, and speaks in a low, gentle tone,
using the best of language—no oaths or slang. He was
willing to talk of himself, but positively declined to say
anything of the movements of the other men. I gave him a
cigar, for which he was very grateful, and arose to smoke
while he conversed. He said he had tried a desperate game
and lost. They were rough boys and used to rough work,
and must abide by the consequences. He was inclined to
think Haywood was more frightened than brave. He was
in the bank, and said the shooting of the cashier was an
impulse of passion on the part of the man who shot him.
He said they all deeply regretted it. They could have
picked off many citizens, as all were dead shots, but did
not desire to do murder. He would not say who shot Haywood. He said the witnesses in Northfield undoubtedly
knew. This was in answer to the question: Did the robber
killed yesterday shoot him? Of course, he regretted his
situation, but all the chances were weighed before starting
in. He had looked over the other banks before deciding,
and knew all about those in the large places, and wished
now he had undertaken one of them, as the chance to retreat was much better in a small place. At Shieldsville they
frightened the boys badly, but did not shoot to kill any-

body. They could have easily shot several. They staid in the woods about Kilkenny Thursday night, when they crossed the ford at Little Cannon. They knew the guards had run, but did not know how many. They moved back into the woods, but started soon to make a crossing before the guards were reinforced. They camped Friday night where the horses were found. They left at daylight, made a little headway, stopped on a sort of a peninsula, probably half a mile from the German church, but part of a day. They made a fire and took comfort. They shot a pig and a calf, both in the head, but they refused to die, and they dare not fire much. They pushed on Sunday night until midnight, and camped in Marysburgh. They heard the church-bell strike six, and thought it was a mile away. They made a fire there and had a good meal of corn and potatoes. Monday they made good headway. At night they camped in a field in the bushes. Twice they were alarmed by people passing near, though they did not go to Indian Lake, as supposed by Sheriff Davis. They said Dunning took a solemn oath not to reveal having seen them. They would not have shot him under any circumstances, and did not tie him in the woods from human feelings, as they feared he would not be found, and would die there. When passing through Mankato the steam-whistle of the oil-mill blew midnight, and startled them. They hid awhile and then passed on, and did not hear or see the guards at the bridge. After crossing, they got four watermelons and had a feast. He said they intended to call around some day and pay the gentlemen for them. They got two old hens and one spring chicken at a house near by, and in fifteen minutes would have had a good breakfast, but they were alarmed by shouting, either of men on the railroad train or by pursuers. They saw one man looking for boottracks, but did not think they were pursuers, but ran up a bank. It was the closest call they had. They did not cross the Blue Earth river then, but did during the day. They then kept on through the woods. Two men then left, and, as the pursuit was directed after them, they had an easier time. He blamed himself for the capture, as he was overcome by drowsiness and insisted on remaining in the field, while the others wished to keep on. They would not leave him; if they had gone half a mile they would not have been caught. He declined saying anything about his previous life. He said they had no regular leader. Every man expected to do his work, whatever it was.

"His wound is in the elbow joint of the right arm, the joint being fractured, and he cannot straighten the arm nor control the fingers. He is very polite; talks when questioned, but not obtrusive, and is so mild-mannered that he would make a good impression on anybody. He shows much gratitude for his good treatment, and fears to give trouble. He says they were all tough, and could have endured much longer. He insisted that it was his own fault that they were captured, as his lagging gave them away. He says the men who captured them were brave fellows.

The dead bandit is a man of very marked physiognomy, coal black hair, whiskers, moustache and eye-brows. His face shows great determination. He must have been killed instantly. On his body were found a compass, state map and pocket-book, with $5. Two of the others had the same amount, and James Younger had $150. Cole had a pocketbook and compass. None had watches. Their clothes were terribly used up. All were well supplied by the citizens. Bob says the coats found in the camp at Mankato belonged to him. They were making due west as near as possible— he would not say where to. Around the face of the dead man flowers had been placed by some lady, and others are scattered on his breast. The swollen features present a horrible sight. Barton had agreed to take the prisoners to St. Paul, but since arriving he has changed his mind, and will proceed directly to Faribault by way of Mankato, leaving here at 5:45 A. M. The body of the dead robber goes by the same train to St. Paul to be embalmed. The trip will be hard on the wounded men, particularly the one shot in the jaw. He suffers much. The doctors here object to moving him, but the men are plucky and will go all right. The town is full of people, but all quiet. No one is admitted to the hotel, which is strongly guarded. When found, the robbers had pieces of underclothing tied on their feet in place of stockings. Cole Younger's toe nails fell off when his boots were removed. He told the doctor he did not care for himself, if dead all would be over in five minutes; was anxious about his brother, and told him to cheer up. He asked the doctor if he would die. While his wounds were being dressed he did not flinch nor move a muscle. He says that when the two comrades left they gave them most of the money, watches, rings and valuables, thinking their chances best."

Another Interview with the Robbers.

The editor of the St. Peter *Tribune* went to Madelia Thursday, and from an extra issued yesterday we extract the following account of an interview with Bob Younger:

He is a man fully six feet high, well built, sandy complexion, and has a pleasant face. We should pick him out of any crowd as a kind-hearted man whom we should expect would grant a favor readily. He conversed freely and answered most of the questions put to him without apparent reserve.

He admitted that the party were engaged in the Northfield robbery, and in reply to our question why they killed the cashier, he said: "It was a d—d fool trick." We asked him if they hadn't a rough time in Minnesota, and he replied that "he had never been in anything like it before." We also asked him why they selected the Northfield bank to rob in preference to others. His reply was that they thought there was more money to be had there—that in Mankato there were three banks and the money was too much divided. In St. Peter he thought they wouldn't have got much.

A Madelia lady called to see him and told him she was glad he fell into Christian hands, and would be well taken care of, and he said he was very grateful for it, but could not say he deserved it.

"Circumstances," he said, "sometimes make men what they are. If it had not been for the war I might have been something, but as it is, I am what I am."

Cole Younger said to the sheriff:

"Are you the sheriff?" and he replied, "Yes."

Cole then replied: "You will get the reward without doubt, but I want to ask one favor of you. If any of them cowardly sons of b—s of detectives come here don't let them in to see us; I don't want to see them nor have to talk to them."

He also told Mr. Estes that if they had chosen they could have shot him and several others, but did not desire to kill any more than they could help, although if they had seen any of the blue-coated police after them they would have picked them off, for they claim they can shoot with accuracy four hundred yards.

Soon after their wounds were dressed, Cole Younger seemed to be soliloquizing to himself, and was heard to say, "I don't believe it—I don't believe it." Upon being asked what he did not believe, he continued: "Byron says, 'Death is the end of all suffering—the beginning of the great day of nothingness;' but I don't believe it."

Among other things learned from them, they stated that the man Dunning, whom they made captive on the 13th near Shaubut's if he had a spark of manhood, would never, after the solemn oath he took, have exposed them. They say they passed through Mankato Wednesday evening, the 13th inst., and the whistle at the oil mill was blown just as they were going by. They supposed they were seen and the whistle was to give the alarm, so they went in back of the mill. They say they have never before been taken prisoners —not one of them.

Capt. McDonough, Chief of Police, St. Louis, accompanied by several others who had known the Youngers several years ago, visited them to identify them. It has been definitely ascertained that Cole and Robert Younger are certainly captured, but James Younger was not in the party. They arrived in St. Paul on Sunday morning, bringing with them accurate descriptions of all of the famous gang, and pictures of most of the gang. They identified at once the body of the dead man as that of Charley Pitts. Those who looked upon the picture they brought of that desperate looking bandit, could not but recognize the resemblance. The dead man is he beyond a doubt. The identification of the other three was not less prompt on arrival here. Two were declared to be Younger boys, and the third man, the one wounded in the mouth, as Al. Carter, a notorious desperado from Texas, who has been with the gang. The Younger boys are Bob and Cole. The men killed at Northfield have been known as Clell Miller and Bill Chadwell, though Chadwell is claimed to be Bill Stiles on very good foundation. It is very likely that the latter name has been adopted for the purpose of outlawry. Mr. Russel, who has known the Younger boys from the earliest time, says before the war they were not remarkably bad boys, but by no means the straightest-laced Sunday school scholars. They became members of Mosby's guerrillas, where they were initiated to deeds of blood and violence, and the life of a bushwacker, and have so lived ever since. The cruelty, the utter disregard of the many bloody rights of war, the cold-blooded atrocity of their deeds made them outlaws, to be hunted after the war's close, and therefore to be outlaws always.

A special dispatch to the Missouri *Republican,* dated at Fairbault, Minnesota, Sept. 26th, says that much excitement prevails over the capture of two of the Younger brothers. It was feared they would be taken from the jail and hung, but good counsel prevailed and no fears of lynching were now entertained. Cole and Bob Younger were not so badly wounded as at first supposed. A company of 75 well-armed men are on guard day and night, and fears were apprehended of a release of the prisoners by their friends.

A special dispatch to the *Globe-Democrat*, St. Louis, of the 26th, says that the James boys, or at least those supposed to be the James boys, are being still pursued, with the hope of yet capturing them.

The editor of the *Mankato Review* interviewed the Youngers, who told him the reason the cashier was killed was that he reached for his revolver and that one of the party killed him, as he supposed, in self-defence. The prisoners waived examination and were committed without bail.

The Younger brothers having plead guilty, have been sentenced to the Minnesota State Prison for the term of their natural lives.